Wilderness
Pleasures

Wilderness Pleasures

A Practical Guide to Camping Bliss

Kevin Callan

The BOSTON
MILLS PRESS

A BOSTON MILLS PRESS BOOK

© Kevin Callan, 2008

First printing 2008

**Library and Archives Canada
Cataloguing in Publication**

Callan, Kevin
Wilderness pleasures : a practical guide
to camping bliss / Kevin Callan.

Includes bibliographical references and index.
ISBN 13: 978-1-55046-497-9
ISBN 10: 1-55046-497-3

1. Camping. I. Title.

GV191.7.C254 2008   796.54   C2008-901407-3

Publisher Cataloging-in-Publication Data (U.S.)

Callan, Kevin.

Wilderness pleasures : a practical guide
to camping bliss / Kevin Callan.
[240] p. : col. photos. ; cm.
Includes bibliographical references and index.

Summary: A guide to getting more out of time
spent out of doors, especially camping. Includes
choosing and planning the right trip; camping
companion harmony; best camping equipment,
gadgets and clothing; close encounters with
wildlife, etc. Sequel to "The Happy Camper."

ISBN 13: 978-1-55046-497-9
ISBN 10: 1-55046-497-3

1. Camping. 2. Outdoor life. I. Title.

796.54 dc22 GV191.7.C355 2008

Published in 2008 by
BOSTON MILLS PRESS
132 Main Street,
Erin, Ontario N0B 1T0
Tel 519-833-2407
Fax 519-833-2195
books@bostonmillspress.com
www.bostonmillspress.com

Editor: Kathleen Fraser
Design & production: PageWave Graphics Inc.

IN CANADA:
Distributed by Firefly Books Ltd.
66 Leek Crescent
Richmond Hill, Ontario L4B 1H1
IN THE UNITED STATES:
Distributed by Firefly Books (U.S.) Inc.
P.O. Box 1338, Ellicott Station
Buffalo, New York 14205

The publisher acknowledges the financial support of the Government of Canada through
the Book Publishing Industry Development Program (BPIDP) for its publishing efforts.

*All photographs by Kevin Callan except as noted. Cover (campfire at sunset),
© RJR, 2008. Used under license from Shutterstock.com; pages 1 and 223, © Johann Helgason, 2008.
Used under license from Shutterstock.com; page 56, Phil Cotton; page 60, Andy Baxter;
page 61, Jim Stevens; page 98, © iStockphoto.com/Tony Tremblay; page 101, © Timothy Large, 2008.
Used under license from Shutterstock.com; Camping icons, © iStockphoto.com/Ceneri.*

Printed in China

CONTENTS

ACKNOWLEDGMENTS

THE FIRST WHO DESERVE THANKS FOR THIS BOOK ARE THE poor souls who choose to travel in the outdoors with me, regulars such as Andy Baxter and Ashley McBride, and especially my wife, Alana, daughter, Kyla, and dog, Bailey. They know full well that anything and everything they do out there has a good chance of being written up by yours truly. I'd like to thank them for their patience, gratitude, expertise, sense of humor and, most of all, their companionship.

Special thanks also to the gang at Boston Mills Press (John Denison, Noel Hudson, Kathy Fraser), not only for being an awesome publishing company but also lifetime friends, and to Joseph Gisini of PageWave Graphics for his design talents.

There's also Jim Stevens at Eureka Packs and Tents, Bill and Anne of Ostrom Packs, Glen Fallis from Voyageur Canoes, the gang at Nova Craft Canoes and the staff at MEC and Wildrock Outfitters. I've bothered them all nonstop for information and also the odd piece of gear during this and every other writing project I've done. I consider all these people friends, not business partners, and thank them.

The inspiration for this book came from James Little, editor of *Explore* magazine, and he deserves credit for it. A couple of years ago, James asked me to be involved in a writing project for the magazine's anniversary issue: "125 Things We Love to Do Out There." Not only did his idea make a wonderful issue, it made one heck of a book idea. I'd like to thank him for that.

And last, but definitely not least, I would sincerely like to thank the wilderness I have tried so desperately to spend most of my life exploring — it has made me who I am today.

The joys of roughing it. Three Narrows Lake, Killarney.

INTRODUCTION

I went along to iron out the wrinkles in my soul.

— Omond Solandt

I SPEND A LOT OF TIME WRITING ABOUT THE UNPLEASANTNESS and discomforts of camping — stories of biting insects, nuisance bears and bad weather. I'm not sure exactly why. For some reason they're always the first tales to be told when I return from a trip. I guess, truth be told, misadventures usually make for better narratives. But what gets me out there in the first place, and what keeps me going out, is definitely not the discomfort. The pleasures of wilderness travel have always been the main attraction for me and, I have to assume, except for a few masochists, the same goes for most other campers out there. There are many ways to get comfortable out there without spoiling the experience. That's the reason behind this book. I thought the time was due for me to highlight the good things, not the bad. Or find the good in the bad. Call it an act of responsibility if you will — this is my way to tell people who haven't gone camping before about the many wonders waiting for them out there, and a way to strike a chord with others who have already gone and experienced them.

Don't get me wrong. I'll still come back and tell tales of grueling trips, and enjoy every minute of it. But there are moments when we all need to consciously seek out and then recall feelings of delight, happiness and contentedness. Times when just the smell of a pine tree, the sound of a loon call, the touch of a cool breeze, anything joyful, really, draws us back to wilderness. That's what this book is all about. A reminder of why we really go out there in the first place.

Seriously, aren't we generally out camping to have fun? I know I am. I get great pleasure out of planning a perfect trip and traveling with good companions; I enjoy my moments of solitude; I'm delighted when mixing a good martini or baking the perfect s'more; I'm jealous of others who have packed along better luxury items or own a more technically advanced camp gadget but proud of my own homemade gear; I'm obsessed with the idea of making love in a canoe at midnight or taking an early morning skinny dip; and I'm absolutely thrilled to spot a bear out on a trail, and even more elated to spin a tale about the close encounter when I return home.

There are, without a doubt, a lot of pleasures to be derived from heading out into the great outdoors, and I greatly anticipate my next trip because I enjoyed the last one. This is the basis of my happiness while camping, and my contentment in life in general. It's what this book is all about — the pleasures found while camping.

1

THE ART OF ANTICIPATION
Getting Ready for Your Trip

"I think," said Christopher Robin, "that we should eat all the provisions now, so we don't have as much to carry."

— A.A. Milne, *Winnie-the-Pooh*

I T'S TRUE WHAT THEY SAY, THAT PLANNING A TRIP CAN SOME-times turn out to be better than the actual trip. If you think about it, most campers take months to prepare, researching the route, collecting the proper gear, asking the right people to come along. There is a huge buildup, an obsession formed, and the anticipation of actually leaving can seem overwhelming, especially as the departure date gets closer. Your job becomes monotonous and, oddly enough, busier as the trip draws nearer. I've even felt nauseous, having the same stomach swirls as I did the first time stepping on an amusement ride. Then the trip happens. The letdown is inevitable. It rains continuously; your partner is a jerk the entire time; the bugs are biting: basically, the trip doesn't end up being at all like what you had originally imagined.

Oddly enough, however, the next year you call everyone together again and begin planning the next trip. It reminds me of my wife after she gave birth to our daughter, Kyla. "Never again," she screamed. "It hurts like hell!" Then, the next year she was talking about having another child.

It was actually my daughter, Kyla, who helped me understand why we do such things; that is, why we anticipate a camping trip to the wilderness so much we can become possessed by the prospect. Others have tried to explain the feeling. Edward Abbey said "Because we like the taste of freedom;

Soaking in the solitude. French River, Ontario.

"Just relax for a minute, Dad. I'm busy looking at this pine cone." Kyla connects with nature in Algonquin Park.

because we like the smell of danger." Charles Lindbergh wrote, "In wilderness I sense the miracle of life, and behind it our scientific accomplishments fade to trivia." And Henry David Thoreau made the plausible claim that "In wilderness is the preservation of the world." But still it was Kyla who made it all clear to me. It was while I watched my daughter sit on the forest floor, at the age of two, and gawk at a pine cone for a good twenty minutes. Right then I saw myself as a child doing the same thing, and it reminded me of why I now like nature so much. She was doing as I once did; Kyla was reconnecting with nature. But more than that, she was reconnecting to the place we all originated from — wilderness.

Top Ten Songs to Listen to Before You Go

- "Poems, Prayers and Promises," John Denver
- "Early Morning Rain," Gordon Lightfoot
- "Shield," David Hadfield
- "Wood Smoke and Oranges," Ian Tamblyn
- "Les Voyageurs," Mike Ford
- "I'm Gonna Be (500 Miles)," The Proclaimers
- "The Rodeo Song," Garry Lee and Showdown
- "One Bourbon, One Scotch, One Beer," George Thorogood
- "Dancing Queen," ABBA
- "Cat's in the Cradle," Cat Stevens

Top Ten Songs NOT to Listen to Before You Go
(or you'll have them in your head the entire trip)

- "We Built This City (on Rock and Roll)," Jefferson Starship
- "Karma Chameleon," Boy George/Culture Club
- "Blowin' in the Wind," Bob Dylan
- "Everybody Wang Chung Tonight," Wang Chung
- "Barbie Girl," Aqua

- "Pour Some Sugar on Me," Def Leppard
- "Funky Town," Lipps Inc.
- "Ring My Bell," Anita Ward
- "YMCA," Village People
- "Mr. Roboto," Styx
- Anything by Elton John after 1972

It's difficult to grasp for some of us, but we all were born from wilderness, and the more our lifestyles take us further and further away from it, making us more and more "civilized," the more desire we have to revisit it. Planning a trip back to our birthplace, to familiarize ourselves with it, is the first step to rekindling our affections. Planning sessions are generally full of enthusiasm. We all imagine ourselves as the best campers, with the best equipment, and we dream of trips where we have the most sublime sleeps, the sweetest-smelling tent companions, the most fabulous weather, the greatest number of animal sightings, the best fish fry-up, the most perfect campsites, the easiest portages. And we all dread the moment when it's over and we're forced back to our unnatural world.

We all dread the moment when the camping trip is over and we're forced to go back to our unnatural world. Author and wife, Algonquin's Catfish Lake.

Inspirational Movies to Watch Before You Go

- **The Yearling** (1946) — Set in the wilds of Florida after the Civil War. A young boy takes in an injured fawn. It's not as sad as *Old Yeller* (1957), but keep a couple of Kleenex boxes beside you just in case.

- **The Long, Long Trailer** (1954) — Lucille Ball and Desi Arnez play newlyweds traveling the open road with their trailer, before we called them RVs. Any RV owner will definitely relate to all the calamities but the funniest scene has to be when Lucy's rock collection rolls around while Desi tries to drive up a steep mountain slope.

- **My Side of the Mountain** (1969) — A young boy leaves home in New York to live in the mountains just as his literary hero, Henry David Thoreau, did.

- **Jeremiah Johnson** (1972) — A mountain man's quest for life as a hermit in the wilderness. Haven't we all wanted to live like Robert Redford at some time?

- **The Life and Times of Grizzly Adams** (1974) — The story was loosely based on the life of a trapper, John Capen, who escapes to the wilderness after being wrongly accused of a murder and then befriends a grizzly bear cub. The movie spawned a television series — until the main actor, Dan Haggerty, got busted for cocaine use.

- **Meatballs** (1979) — Wacky hijinks of camp counselors, including comic genius Bill Murray, highlight pranks and chasing girls more than a love of the woods — but it's still worth watching again.

- **Continental Divide** (1981) — John Belushi is a hard-nosed Chicago journalist covering a story on an eagle researcher. He falls in love with her and with the mountains she calls home.

- **The Man from Snowy River** (1982) — Filmed in the mountains of Australia. It is more about a boy becoming a man than it is about wilderness values, but the scenery is unforgettable.

- **Never Cry Wolf** (1983) — A government biologist is sent to the far north to study the "menacing" wolf population and learns of their true benefit to nature and of the menacing nature of man himself.

- **Black Robe** (1991) — Follows the life of a 17th-century Jesuit priest as he is escorted through the wilderness of Quebec.

- **Without a Paddle** (2004) — Three young men go on a camping trip to fulfill a childhood promise to one another. The trip goes horribly and hilariously wrong.

- **The Last Trapper** (2006) — Norman Winter plays himself as one of the last traditional trappers living in the interior of the Yukon. The scenery captured on film is stunning but Norman makes a far better trapper than actor.

- **Into the Wild** (2007) — Based on a true story. The movie follows Christopher McCandless who, after graduating from university, gives up his "possessions" and hitchhikes to Alaska to live in the wilderness but ends up dying alone. The movie is good, but read the book written by Jon Krakauer first.

Movies to Avoid Watching Before You Go

- **Man in the Wilderness** (1971) — Set in the early 1800s. Trapper and guide (Richard Harris) gets mauled by a grizzly bear and left for dead by his fur-trading buddies. He doesn't die and seeks revenge.

- **Deliverance** (1972) — Based on the book by James Dickey, this classic in which rednecks rape poor Ned Beatty while he and his buddies are out on a canoe trip started Burt Reynolds' career and almost ruined Beatty's. Your friends will definitely hum the familiar banjo tune when they hear you're going camping.

- **Grizzly** (1976) — Came out a year after *Jaws* and was suppose to do to camping what *Jaws* did to swimming in the ocean. Not sure it did.

- **Friday the 13th** (1980) — You'll no longer dream of being a camp counselor after watching this.

- **Redneck Zombies** (1987) — Chemical waste dumped in the woods gets mixed up with a redneck's moonshine, making it no longer safe to wander in the woods.

- **Alive** (1993) — Rugby team takes drastic measures to survive after their plane crashes in the Andes. Human butt cheeks are the first part they choose to eat.

- **The River Wild** (1994) — Meryl Streep deals with armed thugs and wild rapids. The rivers were a little less crowded the year this film came out.

- **Gerry** (2002) — Matt Damon and Casey Affleck run around lost and confused in the desert (shot in Argentina, Death Valley and Utah's salt flats). Not good.

- **The Edge** (1997) — Two men (Anthony Hopkins and Alec Baldwin) try to survive in the wilderness after their plane crashes and a grizzly stalks them; actually, there were three men but the first guy (unknown actor, of course) gets eaten by the grizzly shortly after the plane crashes.

- **The Blair Witch Project** (2001) — Surprisingly terrifying. A cheap but very effective movie about a group of young campers haunted by a witch while roaming the dark woods. The tent scene will have you spooked for months after.

- **Wolf Creek** (2005) — Just when you thought it was safe to go in the woods again. . . . Three young pals head out hiking in the Australian Outback's Wolf Creek National Park. When their car doesn't start, they seek help from a local bushman, and that's when the real trouble begins.

The movie *The Blair Witch Project* scared me silly.

DOING THE RESEARCH

I'm forty-four years old, which means I grew up before text messaging, Facebook, blogging, Yahooing and Googling. I'm Generation X, not Y. I grew up without the aid of an ATM machine, didn't have a credit card in high school, still can't believe they let you use a calculator instead of a slide rule in math class, and actually wrote real letters with pen and paper instead of e-mails to friends and family. What I'm getting at is that planning a camping trip with the aid of a computer hasn't come naturally to me.

Nowadays you can just surf the web and find out everything you ever wanted to know — or might want to buy — in a matter of minutes. Before the internet came knocking at my door, I did all my research on possible routes by mailing out letters to government agencies or phoning up other trippers who had gone before me. Other tidbits of information on, for instance, new camp gadgets available or great campfire recipes, were gathered from books at the public library or through magazine and newsletter subscriptions. The entire process would take months.

When my students at the college I have taught at for close to twenty years laughed at me fumbling through my lectures, I knew that to teach them anything I had to keep with the times and the technology, even stay ahead of them if I could. But now it's second nature for me to surf for information. Before a trip I'll Google, read blogs, and text message my trip partners. I haven't mailed out a letter in years.

"I think we should go here, Dad. Fewer portages means more toys can be packed along." Kyla plans her first canoe trip.

A bookshelf full of dreams…

Yes, the age of postage stamps and friendly government officials sending you free up-to-date information is history. But the world wide web has become one of the best sources for gathering information and advice on where to go, what to pack, and even who to go with. There are on-line dating sites specifically aimed those who want to find someone compatible both in a canoe and in the bedroom. And oddly enough, there are sites dedicated to solo trippers who want to share with others their dislike of traveling with other people. As in any sort of endeavor, you will find evidence of questionable ethics, but I suggest you look for the good bits. Take full advantage of the guy who, instead of enjoying the outdoors, has spent countless hours in his basement logging information on his website just so you can cut and paste and use it in seconds. It may be that he's a traveler-in-waiting, and will be out there with you some day.

Of course, it's important to note that, as with books and magazines, you can't believe everything you read on the internet. Don't let it be your only source of information. (I still visit the library on a weekly basis.) I also have one strict rule set for myself. When I'm prepared to go out, the computer technology that got me there stays home. I am horrified by the news that the number one complaint campground owners receive from their clientele nowadays is that they can't hook up to the web directly at their site. I'm all for comfort and convenience in camping, but there is a time and a place… Maybe it is my age, but the day a campground offers free hookup to the web like a hotel chain does is the day I stop making a reservation at the campground.

Some of My Favorite Sites
(or at least the ones I check out when I'm supposed to be working)

www.barefooters.org
Walking barefoot for hikers is rumored to offer the same sense of freedom that skinny dipping does for paddlers. And this site proves it, detailing the laws that allow you to walk into public places shoeless and providing a list of footwear-free events and more.

www.pbs.org
No, this is not a boring site. The Public Broadcasting System's home page offers some stunning on-line videos, expedition journals and audio/video podcasts.

www.geocaching.com
The sport of geocaching — searching out hidden items with the aid of given GPS coordinates — is huge right now. If your interest is piqued, check this site out.

www.dancewiththetrees.com
The act of climbing in trees and then camping up in the canopy is on the rise. The owners of this site promote the sport to kids and adult groups.

http://bestthike.com/blog
Never a dull moment on this site; it's got updated information on gear, plus trail diaries, maps and photographs.

www.thebackpacker.com/trailtalk
Extremely useful chat forum for gathering information and advice, as long as you can sift out the people who have nothing else better to do than rant on some chat forum.

www.paddling.net
This is an all-purpose site for canoeing and hiking trips, tips and general information. The chat forum is huge but my favorite features are the articles and monthly columns written by outdoors writers (including yours truly).

www.myccr.com
Similar site to paddling.net but Canadian based. But since everyone in the world seems to want to paddle in Canada, it fits a lot larger audience.

www.canoestories.com
Fantastic first-person accounts of canoe trips in Northern Minnesota and Ontario, Canada. This one is majorly addictive.

www.surviveoutdoors.com
Survive Outdoors covers it all, which may be its only downfall. The site even covers information on the bubonic plague. The information on dealing with hypothermia and heat stroke alone makes the site worth wading through.

www.wilderness-survival.net
This is cool. You get to take a survival skills test based on a U.S. Army survival guide.

www.weather.com
Yes, you can check out the weather where you're about to travel. But that's not all the Weather Channel online provides. It gives you ideas on outdoor destinations, safety tips for dealing with nasty weather, and free customized wireless phone weather reports to check out while out on the trail.

www.naturistsociety.com
One of the biggest sites for finding likeminded outdoorsy soul mates; just don't get it confused with www.nudistsociety.com — unless you're into that kind of thing.

www.gayoutdoors.org
Like the preceding site, but with a twist.

www.sheclimbs.org
For women only. SheClimbs is an organization dedicated to women who love to climb. The links, for instance, to Women's Wilderness Institute, seem to offer more than the main site itself.

www.solotripping.com
This site is geared toward adventurers — mostly paddlers — who like to travel alone. It has things other sites have: gear reviews, outdoor tips, related links, trip accounts. But it also has a chat forum which is usually full of members discussing the trials of traveling with other people. The odd thing is the banter is shared with other people. Shouldn't a true solo site be a little less sociable?

www.hikewithyourdog.com
The foundation of this site is a list of dog-friendly hiking trails (American only). Extras are good, including information on dog regulations and safety tips for traveling in the outdoors with your best friend.

www.fitnesstravelgear.com
Fitness Travel Gear provides reviews (and yes, opinions) on various outdoor gear. The reviewers are outdoor writers and general do-it-alls; thankfully, they don't sound like know-it-alls.

www.thegearjunkie.com
Freelance travel writer Stephen Regenolds puts gear through the ultimate test and shows his findings in text and video. This is definitely a site worth checking out.

http://gorp.away.com
Travel portal Away and *Outside* magazine teamed up to provide one big package, from skills to destinations. You can even book your next outdoor trip online right from the site.

Ottertooth.com
This site covers only the Temagami region of Ontario, Canada. But there are lots of tidbits to spice it up, including past issues of the newsletter *Che-Mun* (a journal dedicated to Canadian wilderness canoeing) and trip notes from members of Keewaydin, the world's oldest canoe-trip operator.

Doing the research is half the fun.

"I think we should have gone left at the big boulder, not right at the pine tree."
Bill Ostrom points out our error in navigation on Northern Ontario's Kopka River.

MAP AND FLAP PARTIES

There's no map to human behavior.
— Bjork

The wife of one of my regular canoe partners is a member of an active local club called Stitch and Bitch; she and a few girlfriends get together every second winter Friday to knit sweaters and chat about their lives over wine and cheese. That gave me and my buddy an idea; we started up our own club — Map and Flap — where we meet on alternate Fridays to look over maps, yak about our next outing or reminisce about past trips over beer and pizza.

Maps create dreams; that's why we appreciate them so much. A cluster of contour lines represent a hill to climb; a ribbon of blue is a river waiting to be run down; dotted islands across a sprawling lake contain perfect places to pitch a tent; an isolated pond is that place of solitude you've desperately been seeking out. Maps contain our future adventures and past misadventures, which is why I've decorated my office walls with them. They help inspire me while writing and sometimes give me an excuse to dream the day away, glancing over the penciled comments posting nasty rapids, long portages or picture-perfect campsites. Squashed mosquitoes even decorate some; others contain a moldy scent to remind me of an unplanned dump in a stretch of whitewater.

Most Notable Maps

- A 3,500-year-old clay tablet detailing walls, gates and palaces of the town of Nippur, in what is now Iraq.
- Drawings produced by Leonardo da Vinci, including a map of Tuscany and the Chiana Valley.
- Gemma Frisius' mid-1500s world map, showing the first explanation of the principles of triangulation.
- Gerard Mercator's late 1500s production of the first globe.
- Ottoman Empire map from the 17th century showing the Nile River flowing through Egypt, but with the south arrow rather than the north on top.
- Des Barres' four-volume edition atlas *The Atlantic Neptune*, consisting of sea charts showing the east coast of North America from the St. Lawrence River to Florida and the Gulf of Mexico, which revolutionized mapmaking in the 1770s (and recently sold at a New York auction for $700,000).
- John Spilsbury's 1760 world map (including four, not six, continents), which was cut up and became the first ever jigsaw puzzle.
- Charles Lindbergh's annotated map carried with him during his historic flight from New York to Paris.
- Sketches of author J.R.R. Tolkien's fictional Middle-earth.

So many lakes, so little time. Kip Spidell scans possible canoe routes through Ontario's Algonquin Park.

Topographical maps provide the best two-dimensional view of a third-dimensional world. Many parks and protected areas offer visitors a personalized map of the landscape, but a true topographical map provides the most features. The detail of each topographic map depends on its scale; the smaller the scale, the less detail that is shown. Scales range from 1:10,000 to 1:100,000. For back-country use the most common scale is 1:50,000, meaning 1 cm (³⁄₈ in.) on the map is equivalent to 500 m (1,600 ft.) on the ground. This scale covers the most ground per map and still has enough suitable information, saving you a lot of money in the long run. However, if you require more detail on a specific area (for instance, a long series of rapids or cliff face), use the 1:25,000 scale.

Apart from marking the location of lakes, rivers, rapids, falls, roads, trails and other natural and manmade objects, the most useful information that can be obtained from a topographic map is the topography of the land you are traveling on. The wavy brown lines on the map, the contour lines, do just that. Each line marks where the position of the land is above sea level. Every fifth contour line, called an index contour, has the elevation marked somewhere along its length. The vertical height between each interval is usually 10 meters (approximately 50 ft.). So the closer the lines are together the steeper the grade. Also, the direction a creek or river is flowing is determined by having the closed ends of the contour lines (the tip of the "V") point upstream.

The original information for topographical maps was obtained by aerial photos, most of which were taken in Canada and the United States between the 1930s and 1960s. When you think about it, not only is that a lot of flight time, it's also a long time ago when the photos were taken. The maps are routinely updated, but you can never count on complete accuracy. A case in point: a group of American paddlers traveling the Missinaibi River in northern Ontario noted the portage around the 40-foot Thunderhouse Falls was marked on the right on the map. It's actually on the left. Two of them drowned.

It's also possible to become somewhat obsessed with using maps. I have a tendency to check my whereabouts a little too often, and my regular canoe partner constantly reminds me of that. He's caught me referring to the map rather than the actual landscape stretched out in front of us far too many times, and during our last trip together he finally rebelled. It was when I checked the position of some rapids while we were in the midst of paddling through them. After that he hid the map from me for two full days and insisted I travel not knowing our exact location to teach me a lesson. It worked. I have no idea what lake or river we paddled after that, but it was the most scenic landscape I can remember ever experiencing. It was also our main topic of conversation during our last Map and Flap gathering.

LIGHTWEIGHT AND FANCY FREE

It seems the older campers become the lighter they want their packs. Problem is, with age also comes the desire to be comfortable. And unfortunately these two pleasures generally don't go hand in hand. That's not to say that you should give up on the dream of packing nonessentials and still floating like a feather down the trail. You just have to plan properly.

Brutal analysis of each piece of gear that goes into your pack is your first step. Equipment you take along should be placed under three main categories: essential, just-in-case, and unnecessary but desirable comfort items.

There's no messing around with the essentials, except you should look into items that are multifunctional. For example, duct tape is vital for any repair kit but can also be used as moleskin or fire starter (it has a very effective burning rate when doused with bug repellent). And generally the manufacturers of critical pieces of gear will make high-end lighter options, but for more money, of course.

There is an art to making everything fit into your pack, and bulk is your worst enemy. The items that usually take up the most volume are the tent, sleeping bag and clothes. All of these should be stored in compression sacks, which are indispensable when it comes to reducing bulk. Also, when purchasing a tent, aim for the smallest and lightest you can afford and spend more quality time huddled under a rain tarp during foul weather. I'd suggest

Lightweight Champion

The most notable lightweight packer was author "Nessmuk" (pen name for *Forest and Stream* writer George Washington Sears), who claimed in his book *Woodcraft* (1920) that his load never exceeded 26 pounds (including canoe). His sage advice: "Go light; the lighter the better, so that you have the simplest material for health, comfort and enjoyment."

Nessmuk's List

Clothing	32 ounces
2 wool shirts, 2 wool pants, 2 wool socks, Hat, Boots, Gaiters	
Sleeping Bag	80 ounces
Waterproofed cotton, 6 x 8 cloth	
Knapsack	12 ounces
Pouch	4 ounces
Sheath sewn in, 2 oz vial of fly medicine, Pain killers, 2 to 3 gang of hooks, Brass wire, Waterproof matches, String, Compass, Copper tacks	
Ditty-Bag	2.5 ounces
4x6 leather, 12 hooks, 4-6 yard lines, Flies, 12 buttons, Sewing silk, Thread, Yarn, Sinkers, Salve, File, Wax, Sewing needles	
Dishes	10 ounces
Tin	2 ounces
Hunting Knife	3 ounces
Cotton Tarp	36 ounces
Canoe	160 ounces
2 days of rations	64 ounces
Pocket-axe	10 ounces
Paddle	16 ounces
	Total: 429.5 ounces

you also store the fly and tent body in separate compression sacks. Not only does this reduce the size overall, it also allows you to keep the continuously wet fly away from everything else in the pack. Choose down-filled over synthetic when shopping for sleeping bags. The down bag is unmatched when it comes to warmth, weight and its ability to be compressed to the size of a miniature football. Just make sure it's also packed in a watertight stuff sack. The amount and type of clothes are a little more complex. Your choice of garments is totally dependent on the season. You can't avoid having to bring an extra fleece, longjohns and a wool toque for spring and fall outings. Remember to choose clothing with the highest possible performance-to-weight ratio. In warm summer conditions, however, you need only pack one extra set of clothes. That's all you'll really need. Just hope for a hot, sunny day halfway through your trip so you can do laundry.

The weight of cookware can really add up, especially for a large group. The problem is that most of what you bring is essential. Items such as a camp stove, fuel, and cooking pots are indispensable. There are ways to limit the weight, however. First, spend the extra money and purchase the lightest stove possible and make good use of a windscreen to reduce your fuel consumption. Second, a cheap aluminum pot set bought at a discount store is far better than one of those new-aged titanium sets. Leave your fork at home. Each person needs only a plastic spoon and a handy Swiss army knife for eating. Scrub pads can also be left at home. They end up becoming a breeding ground for bacteria; a handful of pine needles and sand work just as well and is far more sanitary.

Food itself can add up. But if you keep to homemade dehydrated food for at least 80 percent of your meals you can really reduce the weight of your food pack. This doesn't necessarily take away the taste, either. I've made better dinners out there than in the comfort of my own kitchen. And yes, don't pack your food when you're hungry. Keep estimating portion sizes for ingredients such as rice and noodles to a science.

"Anybody seen my tent?" Kip Spidell shows off his new lightweight tent.

The final and probably best advice is to put every item that you would normally bring along on a trip into your pack. Then weigh the pack on a good-quality scale. Now take everything back out and begin considering which items could be left at home or replaced with a newer and lighter version. Take special note of all those little extras. They can cause a real problem. You don't think they mean much. But when added together, all those gadgets and gizmos can really put on the pounds. Start off by multi-tasking. Each item should have two or more jobs. Also, limit the amount of sunscreen, toothpaste and bug repellent. You'll never go through it all on one trip. So stash smaller amounts in smaller containers or shop for those convenient trial packs. Store-bought first-aid kits tend to contain lots of useless items. Making your own not only reduces the weight but yields a much better kit. A repair kit can be made of duct tape and one of those handy multi-tools. A pocket-size disposable camera can easily replace a 35 mm single-lens reflex camera if you're just taking photos to share with friends and family. A small orienteering compass is just as good as a Global Positioning System if you're traveling in a well-used area. A monocular can easily replace binoculars. A paperback novel is better than a cumbersome field guide. Light Emitting Diode (LED) headlights are far superior to cheap flashlights that need extra bulbs and batteries.

ROUTES LESS TRAVELED

Outdoors enthusiasts are becoming more and more desperate to get away from the crowds and find their own Garden of Eden. Of course, the problem is that the numbers of campers trying to escape other campers has increased two-fold in the past few years and it can become insanely busy at times out there. I remember traveling in the Boundary Waters one summer and passing 112 paddlers on a short portage and then counting 226 canoes and kayaks crossing the adjoining lake. That's crazy!

Top Five Most Crowded Wilderness Retreats in North America

- **Grand Canyon National Park,** Arizona, 5 million visitors
- **Yosemite National Park,** California, 3.5 million visitors
- **Olympic National Park,** Washington, 3.2 million visitors
- **Rocky Mountain National Park,** Colorado, 3.1 million visitors
- **Yellowstone National Park,** Wyoming, 3 million visitors

You definitely have to work a little harder to get away from the crowds.
Anne Ostrom, Wabakimi Provincial Park.

It's a Catch 22 for me, though, since I write guidebooks for a living. I promote areas and then curse myself when they become too busy a few months after the book becomes published.

Take Ontario's Algonquin Provincial Park, for example. My wife and I recently headed out to what's perceived to be a more remote section of the park for a canoe trip. We never imagined it would be so crowded. We joined the lineup of 36 canoes that cluttered the take-out of the portage leading into the first lake (North Tea). And to think that Alana and I had decided to paddle this part of the park because we naively thought it would be less busy than any of the southern access points. It wasn't this busy when we first paddled it! Of course, that was before I wrote the guidebook on the park and promoted the scenic splendor of this very route. What had I done? Had I gone too far? Had I become a "wilderness pornographer?"

Writing carries with it some responsibility. Though the intent is to share, promote and sometimes save a wild area, there are times when it feels as if you've actually betrayed a place by helping paddlers love it to death. There are days when I feel like hiding my head in the sand. I've had fellow canoeists shun me at parties after I've written up one of their "secret" spots; I've had cottage owners threaten to "shoot me between the eyes" if I ever write about "their" lake again; I've even witnessed a group of anglers burning one of my books which made mention of the "possible" fishing on a particular lake. And for a moment, while Alana and I waited patiently to use the portage into North Tea Lake, I thought maybe a book-burning party might not be such a bad idea.

However, as we moved forward for our turn to pull out at the portage, I couldn't help but notice that people in the canoe directly ahead of us, a mom and dad with two children, were equipped with my guidebook on Algonquin Park. It was laid out in front of the youngest member (a preteen daughter) with points of interest dog-tagged all through the chapter on North Tea Lake. In conversation with the family, Alana and I discovered it was their very first interior trip, a trip they had decided on after purchasing "some guy's guidebook." I was ecstatic. This family was a reason for me to continue on and promote and possibly save wilderness areas for our future generations. Heck, the daughter even allowed me to go first on the portage because I was loaded down with a heavy pack and an eighteen-foot canoe.

But it's a roller-coaster life. Two seconds later my crotch was suddenly smacked with the wide end of a paddle. A woman traveling the other way on the trail shoved her way through all of us, telling me especially to "get out of her F#@* way." I'll never forget her, dressed in a T-shirt that read "Damn the Dietitian," and carrying only a broad-blade paddle…and a copy of *A Paddler's Guide to Algonquin*. I yelped in pain, jumped off the trail, and watched as she broke every bit of portage etiquette.

So you see, finding the most popular peaks to climb, trails to hike or rivers and lakes to paddle has become easier because of people like me. However, there's a special talent needed to locate the places less traveled, because everyone who knows about them is still reluctant to give them up.

"The best part of the trip is we haven't seen anyone else in days." Scott Roberts rejoices in the remoteness of Northern Ontario.

Best Wilderness Landscapes to Explore in North America*

- **Red Rock Country, Sedona, Arizona**
  Hollywood's most filmed landscapes when depicting the real west; over 100 movies and television shows have been made here.

- **Upper Mississippi River**
  Every bend in the river reads like a chapter in American history.

- **Appalachian Trail, Great Smoky Mountains**
  Best place to view changing colors of autumn.

- **Rocky Mountains, Colorado**
  John Denver sang about the beauty of it. . . enough said.

- **Boundary Waters, Minnesota**
  Over a million acres, and when combined with its neighboring Canadian park, Quetico, offers over 2,000 miles of paddling routes.

- **Nahanni River, Canada's Yukon/Northwest Territory**
  Legendary Canadian filmmaker and canoeist Bill Mason chose this river to be his last to travel down before he died of cancer (1988).

- **Moise River, Quebec**
  Known as the Nahanni of the East, it was the backdrop for the classic how-to book *The Complete Wilderness Paddler*.

- **West Coast Trail, British Columbia's Vancouver Island**
  Rated as one of the most challenging and worthwhile hiking trails in the world.

- **Lake Superior's North Shore**
  Members of the Group of Seven came here to capture on canvas the true character of Canadian wilderness.

* According to *National Geographic Traveler* magazine

There's an art to finding secret spots and exploring them before anyone else.

First off, once you've located a spot, don't be talked into keeping to the trail. Some of the best mountainsides to clamber up or lakes to fish are just over the next hill, far away from the herds of campers following the dotted line on the map. More important, however, is knowing that the less-crowded spots are not found on websites. Information on the internet is just asking for masses of people to congregate there. Go to the library and read historic journal entries of past explorers, old travel logbooks, periodicals, tourism brochures, government travel route pamphlets... Why? Because few people actually go to the library and read through this long-forgotten stuff anymore; they're sitting at home waiting for you to put it up on some website for everyone to see. Instead, do your own research and then keep it a secret as long as possible. Or you could just go to some remote northern town, buy a local a cup of coffee, or better yet a beer, and talk to him until he respects you enough to change his tales of far-off distant secret places to half truths. Then go make his secret yours.

No matter where you are, a big part of the joy of wilderness travel is escaping your average day.

CAMPING IN THE BACKYARD

We're living in a different era, a time where great outdoors adventurers can communicate with us common folk by way of satellite phone or web hookups from the top of Mount Everest or the depths of the Amazon jungle. When you witness such grandeur in exploration it is difficult to feel as if your camping ventures will ever compare. Some people give up camping all together and end up sulking, parked in front of the television watching the "professional" adventurers do what they could only dream of doing.

But lowering your sights and your budget doesn't necessarily mean a bad trip. I know countless expedition writers who ultimately much prefer the familiar, the natural landscape near their home town, than they do far-off places. Richard Frisbie said it best in his book *It's a Wise Woodsmen Who Knows What's Biting Him* (1969): "To the ends of the earth between breakfast and dinner."

Calvin Rustrum

Long before Bill Mason, James West Davidson, John Rugge and Cliff Jacobson, there was Calvin Rustrum. His classic books inspired many tenderfoot campers in the late 1950s and 1960s, especially *The New Way of the Wilderness*. In his *Once Upon a Wilderness* he admitted that after a lifetime of wilderness travel in distant places it was the familiar landscape he most preferred to explore. His books are among the most sought after on eBay.

Top Ten Towns to Live and Play in the Outdoors*

- Asheville, North Carolina
- Haines, Alaska
- Portland, Maine
- Carbondale, Colorado
- Nevada City, California
- Ashland, Oregon
- Sandpoint, Idaho
- Rossland, British Columbia
- Woodstock, Vermont
- Bellingham, Washington

* According to *National Geographic* magazine

A big part of the joy of wilderness travel is escaping the norm of your average day — escaping traffic jams, work deadlines and bad-tempered bosses. Do that in a landscape that's familiar to you and you'll still be recharged by the time you return to the norm. Besides, organizing a big expedition can be stressful. The time, effort and money spent planning can, at times, provoke as much stress as the job you are trying to escape. Traveling locally is not necessarily giving in or lowering your standards; it's a way to create a stress-free holiday.

I live twenty minutes away from a provincial park that contains a large network of paddling routes. I traveled this area extensively before I moved nearby, but after that it seemed I was always heading further north. Just recently, however, I began tripping there again. Life changes when you have a child (and a second job to pay for day care). The amusing part was that I met so many people who had traveled a great distance to visit the park near my home, the same place I was avoiding because it was too familiar to me.

So do yourself a favor the next time life becomes too hectic to organize a trip up Mount Everest or through the Amazon. Get out a road atlas and draw a two-hour driving radius around your hometown. Then, locate a chunk of green on the map and go camp there. It's what the professionals end up doing when they're too old to climb mountains and walk through jungles.

Top Ten Canadian Towns to Live and Play in the Outdoors*

- Rossland, British Columbia
- Gold River, British Columbia
- Parry Sound, Ontario
- Whitehorse, Yukon
- Baie-Saint-Paul, Quebec
- Sussex, New Brunswick
- Dauphin, Manitoba
- Corner Brook, Newfoundland
- Lunenburg, Nova Scotia
- Jasper, Alberta

* According to *Explore* magazine

SPENDING MORE TIME OUT THERE

It was definitely one of the oddest things I've ever experienced while out on a canoe trip — having my quiet morning paddle interrupted by the sound of a Dan Gibson *Sounds of Nature* music CD. I rounded the bend and there they were, a middle-aged couple sitting on their portable lawn chairs, sipping from mini-espresso cups and listening to a mixture of loons calls and symphonic melodies emanating from their waterproof boom box.

My curiosity got the better of me; so, rather than paddle by their camp as quickly as possible, I turned toward shore and paid them a visit, introducing myself with the question: "How long ya out for?"

"Seven hours, maybe eight if we're lucky" was the response.

Apparently this was a weekend outing. They had left the city Saturday morning, got caught up in a traffic jam on the expressway and arrived at the launch area just before dusk. Camp was made at the first available site (ten minutes from the launch) and they were up at sunrise, hoping to pack up quickly and head back on the highway before the traffic got bad.

Tips on Packing for a Longer Trip

- Planning is everything. Know your gear inside out and calculate travel distances for each day.
- Have a "plan B" and a "plan C" in case of emergencies.
- Know where help can be found en route (for instance, outpost fishing camps).
- Plan a rest day every five days.
- Plan at least one day extra for delays due to weather or other unknown circumstance.
- Choose a good partner, one you'll be comfortable and safe with for the duration of the trip.
- Organize a meal plan.
- Majority of food should be dehydrated (except maybe for the first two days), and each meal placed in a separate resealable bag, labeled, and placed in organized sacks labeled breakfast, lunch and dinner.
- Pack vitamin C and multivitamins.
- Take a first-aid course and pack a good, useful first-aid kit.
- Pack a good repair kit.
- Forget the axe or hatchet (which cause many injuries) and just use a folding saw.
- Go to the gym for a couple months beforehand.
- Make a dental and doctor's appointment a few weeks before.
- Rent a satellite phone and know how to use it (programming all the important phone numbers).
- Watch your hygiene and try to stay clean.
- Be well aware of your group's limitations and all agree never to take unnecessary chances.
- Take a camera and a log book.

"I figure we can stay another week out here if we only have three pancakes a morning instead of five." Author and wife try to extend their canoe trip in Quetico.

I never did get up the nerve to ask them about the boom box. Who knows, maybe packing it along was just a kind of insurance, in case they didn't have time to hear the full complement of loons, wolves and white-throated sparrows on such a short trip. Whatever the reason, I came to the conclusion that morning that the world of paddling has undeniably changed. We're definitely working too much, too long, and in need of the intrinsic values of wilderness more than ever before. As proof, look at the history of paddling guidebooks. The ones published in the 1930s had routes averaging a month or two in length. In the 1970s they promoted seven- to ten-day trips. In the 1980s they were reduced to five. Now, the average trip marketed is two to three days.

The problem, however, is that you're not even into a good rhythm until the fourth day. Your addictions to caffeine and fast foods don't begin to loosen their grip until day five. And it's not until the tenth day you're actually at ease with your surroundings out there. Comfort then becomes a relative term.

It turned out that my weekend friends managed to stay one more night on the lake before heading back to the city. I camped across from them and, strangely enough, was pleased as punch to hear a blend of French horns and the fluty call of the wood thrush coming from their campsite. They had obviously reassessed their situation, prioritized their life, and come to the conclusion that staying longer in the woods was worth it — maybe even long enough for the batteries to die in their boom box and the real Sounds of Nature to kick in.

2

GOOD CAMPING COMPANIONS

I'VE ALWAYS BELIEVED THAT THE SECOND-BIGGEST REWARD you get while camping in the woods (the first being the wilderness thing) is the companionship. Sharing your experiences, good or bad, can create lifelong friendships.

Sure, there are always a few losers who can tag along. I had a married man who attempted to have an affair during a trip, until his wife caught him; another man tried to end his life while canoe-tripping with me and his sons; I had a major drug user pump heroin into his veins on another trip and a bunch of snobby business types take off with the canoes while I dealt with a nuisance bear at camp. The list goes on. But generally speaking, I've shared some great times with some great people out there. Sometimes the best are the ones you might think wouldn't be compatible at all. Take my neighbor, for example.

Ashley was just the guy who lived across the road and I never really thought of him as a good canoe partner, mainly because he'd never canoed before. He was always the guy I had a beer with while helping to fix a fence or something.

One day, however, Ashley asked to go on one of my trips, and for some odd reason I said yes. After all, what could happen? At least that was the last thing I said to my wife before heading out the door. By the end of it, I was lying in the tent with a broken foot (jumped into the river and hit a rock). I had no Tylenol and no booze — nothing to ease the pain. I used up all the Tylenol on the second morning after drinking all the booze the first night. What a disaster.

Bailey used to sit up in the front with Alana...and then Kyla was born. Our dog is still quite upset about that.

It was a good place to break a foot, though, if you were so inclined to do so. It was the last lake of the last night of the trip. And I was thankful I wasn't alone. My neighbor Ashley graciously agreed to carry me out.

I felt like an idiot. It was a silly stunt that lacks a good story, except for maybe when Ashley refused to help me out of the water at first because I wasn't wearing a bathing suit and nine female members of the Quebec Nature Federation were camped directly across from us. However, I was okay with hauling myself to shore since he was clad in a tight black Speedo bathing suit. There's just something wrong about being rescued by a guy wearing a Speedo.

I never wear a bathing suit on canoe trips; especially with only male companions. It would be like wearing your underwear in the locker room showers, for heaven's sake. If in fact the girls from Quebec saw us, they may have giggled at my naked body — which would be no surprise to anyone — but they would have definitely been offended by seeing a man in one of those skimpy European "string up the back" Speedos.

It was definitely an odd trip. But I've traveled with Ashley on a few more outings since. He's still a little odd when it comes to swimwear but he's a perfect paddling partner, and a friend for life.

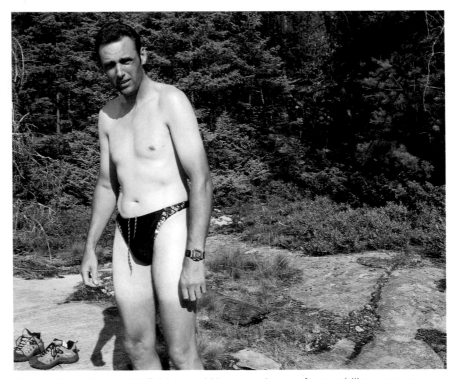

Speedo Man (Ashley McBride) would have made a perfect paddling partner if only he had left his skimpy swimwear at home.

Bill and Anne Ostrom — a rare canoe couple, because they actually get along out there.

Top Ten Characteristics of a Good Partner
(if your partner has half of these, consider yourself blessed)

- Good communicator
- Not selfish
- Does his/her fair share of work
- Dependable
- Humorous
- Has a special skill to share
- Confident of abilities but not arrogant
- Knows his/her limits
- Has good judgment
- Realizes that everyone has his/her own "unique" character

TAKING THE KIDS CAMPING

Okay. It's time to admit it. You're a parent now. Your life is different. It's changed dramatically, actually. And your friends were right when they told you that the days of high-energy and adventurous camp outings are gone, or at least put on hold.

What many friends fail to tell you, however, is that camping trips with children are actually better than the ones before family life. They may not give you as much freedom as you once had, but they certainly are more memorable.

My daughter was six weeks old when she went on her first overnight. My wife and I weren't doing it because we were extreme campers who had a deep philosophical view of introducing children to nature at an early age (even though that's not a bad idea). It was because we simply couldn't deal with being stuck inside with a crying baby anymore and thought being out-doors with a crying baby might be better.

Author Kevin Callan helps daughter Kyla celebrate her third birthday during a two-week camping trip.

Kyla had her third birthday on a twelve-day canoe trip. That was her first real camping trip. All the others before that were weekenders at a not-so-remote lake or a busy campground. Our daughter was ready to take on the longer interior trip before that, but we weren't, especially me. I'm the most paranoid father in the world.

My wife and I learned a lot on that trip. Practical things such as where to camp, distances traveled per day, what to pack, and more important, what not to pack. We also made sure Kyla's time out there was enjoyable (so we could selfishly go out again without her rebelling). But before I go into all of that, there's one thing we learned camping with Kyla that was a surprise. The biggest pleasure we gained by taking our daughter camping was what she herself taught us. Kyla slowed our pace dramatically by spending time looking at things like bugs and plants with the outmost curiosity. It's not that my wife and I didn't do that as well, but we didn't do it as often. Through our more adventurous trips in the past we got caught up in that game of traveling far so we can see more. Tripping with a child brought us back to reality. I've never been so immersed in wilderness, so aware of my surroundings, than on our twelve-day trip with Kyla. I'd have to say that camping with our child did not signify the end of my time in the out-of-doors; it offered a new beginning.

Be Realistic

Know your child's limits. Our three-year-old daughter had a good hour-and-a-half in the canoe before she got fidgety and bored; and that's good in comparison. The average time kids under five can spend in a canoe or hiking a trail is only thirty to forty minutes. Take note that my wife and I got Kyla to that point slowly by going on a half-day outing, then a full day, then a weekend, and so on. If you don't move up the ladder of progress slowly, your child will definitely come crashing down.

All children have different limitations and all parents have various degrees of skill level and stress levels. So don't take the expert's advice on what your child can accomplish out there too seriously; this time, you're the expert.

Your child needs direction out there. Explain everything to them, communicate with them, involve them in the trip, and never treat them like baggage tagging along on "your" trip. Act more like a guide. Travel as fast as the slowest member, have an escape route planned, and depend heavily on repeat business.

When to Take Them

The biggest question asked about taking kids camping, especially in the interior, is how old should they be before taking them. My experience has taught me the earlier the better. A child is easier to handle at the campsite when they are not walking. Once they're walking, the campsite becomes a constant danger zone. Many parents decide to wait until they are a preteen. That's a huge mistake. Preteens do not want to spend time with their parents.

What to Feed Them

Breast feeding offers a huge advantage. But if they're past that stage, then powdered milk may have to do. And don't feel you can't dehydrate baby food. Use a commercial dehydrator or just spread it out on a cookie sheet and dry it in a conventional oven at the lowest temperature overnight. At camp, boil the dried food in a half cup of water and it turns right back to the original baby food. As they get older, pack what they eat at home. Don't depend on them eating exactly what you're eating.

The Diaper Debate

One of the biggest concerns parents usually have traveling with the two-and-under crowd is the diaper dilemma. First, there's the cloth versus disposable debate. Both have their problems. Cloth diapers can be washed and dried at camp, but this means doing a serious laundry every day. Don't rinse them in the lake. Bring a portable basin and make sure to dispose of the contents of diaper and rinse water in the outhouse or at least 30 meters away from camp. Many parents find it much easier to carry disposable diapers, carrying out the used ones in a double-lined garbage bag. I have seen some campers try to burn disposables in the fire pit before leaving their site. The diapers definitely don't burn, however. They just look like big crusty globs of charred plastic goop making the campsite a complete eyesore for the next camper who comes along.

One parent I know recommends the stoop and scoop method. He packs disposables when camping with his one-year-old but lets the child go without diapers or pants for most days at the campsite.

Another idea is to pack along cloth and disposable diapers, cleaning the cloth diapers on sunny days at camp and saving the disposables for the rainy days on the trail.

Don't Be Cheap With Gear

Yes, I know they'll grow out of that sleeping bag or rain suit in a year's time. And I know that even moderate gear is expensive. But don't go cheap or you'll be sorry, like when it turns cold and the zipper of their sleeping bag breaks or it pours down rain the entire trip and the rain suit you bought on sale begins to leak the first day. You should think about gear purchases for them as much as you do for yourself. If you don't have money, then beg, borrow or buy used gear.

In considering when to take children, remember, the younger the better. No teenager wants to go camping with his or her parents.

Where Do They Sit in a Canoe?

We own a 17-foot canoe (I wish it was 18 feet). Our daughter is small enough to sit directly beside my wife in the bow and once in awhile will sit down in front of her. I've seen other parents place one or even two children sitting on the bottom of the canoe in front of the centre yoke. If you have two or more children, eventually the parents will have to split up and steer separate canoes. If you have an older child, you might consider giving him or her a kayak to paddle.

If you wear your PFD then your children will wear their PFDs. Period. Parents who force their child to wear a lifejacket all the time but don't wear theirs will definitely create an issue. And make sure the PFD fits and is comfortable to wear.

Kyla and Mom enjoy a cuddle at the end of a long day.

Portaging

Any portage over 440 yards (400 m) is too long for a child under five. And having them walk it twice won't be easy. Our plan is that my wife walks Kyla over the trail while carrying a pack and Kyla carries her own small pack (it helps to make them involved). When they get to the end they read a story while I return for the second trip.

How to Deal With the Bugs

Be sure to use a mosquito repellent that doesn't harm sensitive skin (Johnson's Skintastic works well). A bug jacket might be a good idea, even a bug tarp. Or better yet, plan your holidays late in the summer when bugs aren't as much an issue. Those "after bite" pens can also help relieve the nasty itch of insect bites.

Where Do They Sleep?

Pack a portable crib for babies and a car seat for inside the canoe. The older kids get to sleep in the same tent with mom and dad until they are old enough for their own tent. Choose a tent one size larger than normal and have a divider between your sleeping area and the kids. Nap time is either spent in the canoe or on shore under a bug shelter. Just make sure they have their nap.

Know How to Answer "Why?"

Our daughter went through the "Why?" stage during a full season of camping and I'll be honest, it drove me crazy. Why are trees green? Why do mosquitoes bite? Why are you so afraid of bears? I answered each one quickly and to the point. But let me tell you, there were many days I secretly wanted to just ignore her questions. But you can't. It would be far worse if they never questioned nature. Let them be inquisitive; after all, that's why you have them camping in the first place.

Be as Creative as a Camp Counselor But Be Responsible

Have games, songs and activities prepared in advance, and know how to make them fun. Kids don't care about how many bird calls you hear or how nice the weather is. They want to play on a beach, go swimming, be told silly stories before bed, burn marshmallows on a stick, feel comfortable and at home. Make a birthday cake for no apparent reason, hand out dollar-store gifts every morning, read them a book at the end of every portage, hand out wacky candy for each camp chore they do, bring musical instruments such as spoons or a harmonica.

If you wear a PFD so will they. Period!

However, you are doing double duty on a camping trip. Not only do you want to entertain them, you also want them to be safe. And you have the sole responsibility to make sure they are safe. It's true that fewer accidents happen on a camping trip than at home, but because you are somewhat isolated on a trip, injuries can be or least seem to be more severe.

Laugh and Don't Show Your Fear

Things will definitely go wrong while on a trip. Count on that. And your phobias (mine are bad weather and nuisance bears) are on high alert when you're with your family. But if you don't laugh at the misfortunes, the moderate ones, at least, or reveal the fears you have of things out there, then they will do the same. Whether you want to admit it or not, you are their role model, and they are little sponges soaking up everything you do and say out there. If you giggle at a tumble on the portage or sing a silly song during a downpour, they will too.

More Tips From My Wife

- Go with a guide if the adults on the trip are novices.

- Make sure everyone in the family wants to go — don't force them.

- Make sure everyone is going for the same reasons. If you are planning a fishing trip but half the family hates fishing, you'll have problems.

- Make sure you and your spouse or other adults communicate well. There's nothing like a bad canoe trip to ruin a perfectly good relationship.

- Planning is crucial — plan your trip ahead of time and leave a map and itinerary behind with friends and family so they'll know where to look if you don't return.

- Allow a lot of wiggle room in the schedule. Half the day is for travel and the rest is to swim, play and find camp.

- Trip with another family with children around the same age. I know our daughter gets bored playing with mom and dad all the time.

- Each child should have his or her own flashlight. It gives a great sense of security as well as a way to play shadow puppets before bedtime.

- Each child should have a whistle clipped to his or her belt and know to use it if he or she happens to wander off the campsite or trail.

- A sunhat should be worn at all times.

- Don't pack along a huge toy box. Allow only one of their favorites. Once out there, children will soon create their own toys from pine cones, rocks and weird-shaped pieces of driftwood.

- Pack plenty of Band-aids and a good collection of soothing words to help heal all the little cuts and bruises that are sure to appear.

- Choose safe campsites. Stay away from steep drop-offs and slippery rocks. Have them wear their PFD along the shoreline and watch for those nasty patches of poison ivy.

DOG PADDLING

This year my "end of the season" paddle ended up in Ontario's Killarney Provincial Park. I usually choose to go solo on my last outing of the year. But this time I decided to ask along three other campers: Andy Baxter, his golden retriever, Monty, and my hyper springer spaniel, Bailey. Andy and I knew we would get along on the trip. We've been paddling together for years. But we weren't sure about Monty and Bailey. Both were canoe dogs who had experienced quite a few canoe trips. But they hadn't traveled together before and Andy and I were a little anxious about squeezing them in the canoe side by side with our pile of gear. As it turned out, both dogs got along. In fact, they complemented one another quite well. Bailey successfully chased the camp mice away from Monty, and Monty retrieved fetching sticks for Bailey. Both dogs even saved us from getting lost during a day hike. We had decided to go ridge hiking and on our return trip to the canoe Andy and I got "confused" about which direction to take. If it weren't for Monty and Bailey leading the way, we'd still be walking the ridges of Killarney.

Bailey and Monty patiently wait for dinner to be served. Ruth-Roy Lake, Killarney Park, Ontario.

"Honest, I can't fetch another stick." Bailey relaxes after a long day on the trail.

Dogs are a strange breed. Some are well behaved and considerate, while others are just a plain nuisance, which is why the question of whether or not you should have them join you on a camping trip is not cut and dry. Much of it depends on the actions of the owners themselves. I witnessed someone's beagle harass a cow moose by leaping out of the canoe and swimming after the poor beast. Half my food pack was once consumed by a golden retriever at the take-out of a portage. At a public campground I saw a poodle that had been leashed to a tree during the night torn apart by a pack of coyotes. I had the displeasure of mistaking an over-friendly and unleashed black Lab for a marauding black bear. And more than once I've set my tent atop a mound of fresh dog doo-doo and didn't realize it until I packed up the next day. I blame these incidents not on the dogs but on the owners themselves. Quite honestly, they have no business having a pet in the first place, let alone bringing them along on a camping trip.

My wife and I have been tripping with our springer spaniel, Bailey, for six years now and believe that the golden rule is to take responsibility for your dog's actions. Chasing animals and leaving feces behind on a campsite is normal dog behavior. But having the owners allow them to do that is not. When we first took Bailey camping, Alana and I made sure she was always with us and was never allowed to wander off. We even leashed her while on busy portages or hiking trails. It wasn't easy training her. Bailey simply loves being off the lead. But by using stern commands (and a few treats), we taught our dog never to leave our side. Now she's better trained while on a canoe or hiking trip than she is at home. It's all a routine for her now — staying still while in the canoe, heeling the moment we spot an animal or bird, heading off the trail to relieve herself, not complaining about having her PFD put on before we run a dangerous set of rapids, waiting for her dog pack to be strapped on before heading down the portage.

We've also built up a routine of watching over Bailey, generally because she doesn't always look after herself. A trip to the vet is always planned before we head out to make sure her shots are up-to-date and she's in good overall health. We pack a first-aid kit specifically designed for dogs. Bailey's regular choke collar is replaced with a glow-in-the-dark nylon collar. I've glued a slab of foam padding on the bottom of the canoe for her to sit on

First-Aid Kit for Dogs

- Ace self-adhering athletic bandages
- Cotton Balls or Q-tips
- Vet wrap bandage, the kind used for dressing a horse's leg
- Sock, great for keeping a foot bandage on
- Gauze sponges
- Liquid Bandage works well on patching mild cuts on pads
- Antiseptic towelettes
- Hydrocortisone one-percent cream
- Rubbing alcohol
- Eye rinsing solution
- Small container of Vaseline
- Hydrogen peroxide, a good way to induce vomiting (1–3 tsp. every 10 minutes until dog vomits)

- Benadryl (1–2 tablets every 8 hours for average-size dog)
- Pepto Bismol tablets (1–2 tablets every 6 hours for average size dog)
- Buffered aspirin (*not* Tylenol or ibuprofen)
- Kaopectate tablets (1–2 maximum strength tablets every 2 hours for an average-size dog)
- Emergency ice pack
- Ear syringe
- Antibiotic ointment
- Bandage scissors
- Tweezers
- Blanket
- Dog's health record and phone number of regular vet

(this gives her a place to call her own and helps to control her while in the boat). I've even attached an umbrella holder on the gunwale to give Bailey some shade while we paddle across a large lake. And rather than put bug repellent directly on her skin, which she'll definitely lick off and make herself sick later on, I'll spray it on a bandana that we tie around her neck. The bandana also helps other campers identify her as a dog and not a bear if they accidentally run into her on the trail.

Speaking of bears, we also don't assume Bailey will keep us safe from them. I know a lot of people who have brought dogs out with them for that specific reason. It's true the bear will most likely think twice about coming into a camp with a dog barking. However, a bear once wandered into our campsite because of Bailey's constant whimpering. It thought she would be an easy meal, I guess. I guarantee that if the bear ever went for Bailey, our dog's instant reaction would be to run right toward us — bringing the bear along with her.

HOW TO MAKE LOVE IN A CANOE

For we Canadians, making love in a canoe beats joining the mile-high club hands down. In fact, ever since and probably long before Pierre Berton wrote "A true Canadian is one who can make love in a canoe without tipping," the sexual act has been attempted all over the country — in lightweight Kevlar, splinter-infested cedar-canvas, and even bum-numbing aluminum Grummans. There's no question most canoeists wish to give it a go. It seems that what's stopping them is some trepidation over what position is best — without tipping, that is. Well, even though Philip Chester once made the claim "Anyone can make love in a canoe, it's a Canadian who knows enough to take out the centre thwart," it turns out that the most preferred position is actually over the thwart!

Embarrassingly, my first time doing it in a canoe was the night before a cover story article I wrote on the subject hit the newsstands. I had written the entire article, submitted it to the editor, and cashed the check for the job — but I was still a canoe virgin, and I was okay with that. It was my wife, Alana, who wasn't going to stand for it. She insisted that I (we) make love in a canoe before the magazine saw the light of day. Doing the act on a moment's notice was a challenge, however. Alana left me to figure out the details while she went upstairs to put our three-year-old daughter to bed.

Actually paddling out on water was going to be impossible, of course. It was too short notice and we live in the middle of a city and we didn't have a babysitter. I first thought a quick substitute would be just to flip the canoe over right where it was being stored on the back lawn. But then I thought about how nosey our neighbors seem to be, not to mention how much the scenario lacked in romantic quality. So instead I put the sixteen-foot boat right through the back window of our house, rested it beside our living room fireplace, placed a couple of glasses of wine on the bow plate, and put a "nature sounds" CD in the stereo.

The mood was set. I sat in the stern seat, wearing only my bathrobe, and waited for Alana to walk downstairs for the big surprise. And a few minutes later she did, but with our daughter in her arms. Kyla had a slight fever and needed a bit more comforting before going to bed.

It was an embarrassing moment for any father. That's a given. But Kyla saved me by immediately asking "Are we going camping, Dad?" Of course I said yes, and then spent a good hour playing camp-out with Kyla and her dolls.

It was love at first sight for Ashley McBride and Sally-Anne.

Canoe Sex Tips

There are a few steps to consider before making love in a canoe. Not all are necessary; just remember to have safe sex out there while doing the nasty — wear your PFD!

Step 1 The best time and place is under a starlit sky, in the middle of a calm lake. It has, however, been done in mid-rapid, while the canoe is beached on shore, and even while the canoe is being stored in the backyard. It's also been known for kayakers to give it a go — unsuccessfully, that is. Wasn't it Caroline Owen who once said "Paddle solo, sleep tandem"? She must be a kayaker.

Step 2 Get the okay from your partner first; surprising them with the idea out in the middle of the lake could quickly spell out disaster.

Step 3 Create the proper mood by lighting candle lanterns at bow and stern, filling your enamel camp mugs with a splash of wine, and placing a sleeping pad in the center of the canoe. . .or just go for a quickie before someone sees you and figures out what you're doing out there.

Step 4 Remove all clothing, of course, including footwear; bare feet ensure a better grip.

Step 5 Consider lashing two canoes side-by-side. It increases stability and — if you're into that sort of thing — invites group sex.

Step 6 End with a quick skinny-dip to cool down.

"What happens at the campsite, stays at the campsite."

To date I'm still a "canoe virgin," and according to my wife I'm also a "complete idiot" for hauling a canoe into the house and thinking she'd be up for a quickie in a boat balanced on a remnant of shag carpet. But the good news is that my daughter thinks I'm the coolest dad ever for bringing in extra props for her dollhouse. She cried the next morning when I took the canoe back outdoors. So did I.

And the thing was, I still had to write about how to make love in a canoe for this book. And my publisher wanted photos. However, the in-house photo shoot didn't really capture what I was hoping it would. Romance under the stars, etc., etc.

With my wife in total refusal mode for being a model at this point, my next plan of attack was to purchase a blow-up doll. This ended up being an even more embarrassing moment in my life. I entered a joke-gift shop at the mall and, since I had Kyla with me and the inflatable women were on display with some rather rude sex toys in the back, I asked the sales clerk to retrieve one for me. That moment a woman from Kyla's daycare wandered into the store and when she stopped to say hello, the clerk yelled out "Which model do you want?"

How awkward. I panicked, of course, and sheepishly replied, "The cheapest one you have in stock." The clerk countered with "The anatomically correct bisexual one it is, then."

I wandered out of the store with my girl/boy doll double-bagged, hoping never to see the woman from Kyla's daycare again, and wondering how on earth I would photograph having sex with an inflatable person with both sex organs while in a canoe. The answer — I had my oddball neighbor agree to pose. Yes, alas, I am still a canoe virgin.

THE ZEN OF SOLO TRIPPING

I travel solo more often than not, so I can see why others would judge me antisocial. Truth is, I quite enjoy the company of others. I hang out with a variety of friends and especially take pleasure in meeting new and interesting people. But for reasons I can't seem to explain, there are times I'd rather be alone.

There are varying kinds of aloneness. Some people need only an hour or two of quiet time; others go for the hermit stage, never wishing to see another human being as long as they live. I'm somewhere in between. A good dose twice a year would suffice, added on to those daily early morning walks to the park with the dog. What I'm talking about is a solid camping trip alone for more than five days but less than ten.

Why not just three days? Well, because no matter who you are and how comfortable you are out there, the first night alone in the tent you're terrified. Believe me, a chipmunk walking past your tent will sound like a bear to you. By day five, though, you're so exhausted worrying about bears each night you end up caring less about them. And by day ten, the thought of a bear breaking through the flimsy nylon tent doesn't cross your mind; after all, if one hasn't gotten you yet, there's little to worry about. More notable, however, is that you've finally become comfortable with your surroundings, and seeing a bear actually becomes a highlight of the trip, not a terrifying experience.

After day ten, though, you begin to miss the social aspects of hanging around other people; you can even get bored of yourself. And the longer you stay out, the more culture shock you'll get when you return.

But is it dangerous traveling by yourself? The answer to this is yes and no. Yes, it is dangerous, or consequentially more dangerous because you're traveling in a seemingly chaotic wild place without a safety net. If something were to go wrong, you'd be on your own to get yourself out. However, when you are traveling alone you are usually so worried about something bad happening that safety becomes a top priority and an injury rarely happens; traveling in groups you have a false sense of security, you are trying to

Notable Solo Ventures

John Muir: In 1867 the man who was later dubbed the first modern preservationist decided to enroll in the "university of wilderness"and set out on a 1,000-mile walk from Indiana to Florida.

Lillian Alling: An immigrant from Russia who grew so homesick living in New York she decided to walk back to her homeland in 1927 and was last seen two years later bartering with the Inuit for a boat to cross the Bering Strait to Asia.

Ella Maillart: A noted Swiss woman who became one of the most amazing travelers of the 20th century, her best overall trip being a journey through Central Asia in the early 1930s from Tien Shan Mountains of Mongolia to the fabled Bokhara.

Colin Fletcher: In 1963 this "compulsive walker" became the first to walk the length of Grand Canyon, below the Rim.

Peter Jenkins: A disillusioned hippie and his dog Copper walked across America, from New York to Louisiana, in 1973 to restore his own faith in his country.

Chris Townsend: A contemporary adventurer and veteran hiker, he was the first to walk 1,000 miles from the Chilkoot Trail in Southeast Alaska to the Richardson Mountains of the Arctic Circle (1990).

Christopher Johnson McCandless: A troubled youth who hitchhiked to Alaska in 1992 and was later found starved to death in an abandoned bus.

Steve Fossett: In 2002, after five failures, he became the first person to circumnavigate the globe nonstop in a hot air balloon. Fossett set many more speed and distance air records but disappeared flying somewhere over Nevada in September 2007 and no trace of his aircraft was ever found.

Ultimately, true wilderness is a place where no humans exist, and being there alone is the closest you're going to get to that place.

keep up with or lead the others, and the chance of an accident is greatly heightened. For example, I broke my foot after blindly jumping into the water while on a canoe trip with a friend. He carried me out to safety and commented after the event that I was lucky not to be traveling solo at the time. My response to him was that if I was alone, I would never have foolishly jumped into the water the way I did. You're going to need a bit of previous experience to survive on your own. The knowledge gained by experiencing mishaps while with a group and learning from your own or someone else's stupidity will stand you in good stead when you go it alone.

What's so good about traveling solo? Well, for starters you can eat what you want and when you want; travel wherever and for how long you like. Basically, you can do whatever you want to do. Planning the trip is even quicker and easier. Your senses are more alive than ever before when alone, and life itself, well, becomes much more meaningful. You also have plenty of time on your hands to be a deep thinker, to study the complexities of nature and get in tune with your natural surroundings. Ultimately, true wilderness is defined as a place where no humans exist, and being there alone is the closest you're going to get to that place.

Best Books to Read Alone

- *Ishmael,* by Daniel Quinn
- *A Thousand Mile Walk to the Gulf,* by John Muir
- *The Lonely Land,* by Sigurd Olson
- *Desert Solitaire,* by Edward Abbey
- *The Starship and the Canoe,* by Kenneth Brown
- *Into the Great Solitude,* by Robert Perkins

"And after the book is read, when supplies run short, it can serve as toilet paper." Alana Callan, Steel River.

WOMEN ONLY, PLEASE

There was a time when the major part of my income came from guiding people on canoe trips. I worked for a base camp in Ontario's Temagami region and spent the summer traveling with a new group of clients every week. Surprisingly, it was my people skills that would make or break each trip, more so than my camping skills. Good group dynamics was the key to surviving each trip.

I guided a real mix of personalities and group combinations. There were high school youths, seniors, juvenile delinquents, married couples, co-ed clusters, women-only retreats and those memorable male-bonding ventures. When it came to choosing the worst and best groups to guide, men were always a nightmare and women were always the most pleasurable. My preference had little to do with me being a sex-crazed twenty-year-old at the time; at least I like to think that wasn't the main reason. My pleasure in guiding women had to do with good group dynamics.

Experience taught me that women seemed to communicate better than men; they had a higher pain threshold than men; they were safer than men; and their personal hygiene always won over men's. Guys, you're going to hate me for saying this, but most of the time you were a pain in ass when it came to guiding you on a canoe trip.

Male trips always turned disastrous. Day one, guaranteed, was spent trying to gather everyone up like a herd of cattle. Each male in the group thought he was better than the other and desperately tried to prove it by paddling faster and harder. We made a lot of distance and it wasn't that much of an issue, at least not until day three or four, when everyone was so exhausted from competing with one another that we would lose ground and fall behind. The more time we had to make up near the end of the trip, the crankier the men became; and with their inability to communicate their feelings, yelling matches or even fist fights became inevitable.

Danger Boy was always alive and well around an all-male group. There were the axe-throwing competitions, cliff jumping, or worse the "my fire is bigger than your fire" contests that always got way out of hand. I don't recall ever guiding an all-male trip without unpacking the first-aid kit.

Constantly challenging my leadership had to be the worst dysfunction, though. Maybe I lack a few male hormones myself due to being brought up with three older sisters, but I never could completely understand why some

Girls rule! Meeting up with camp girls from Widjiwagan in Quetico Park.

Girls still rule. Meeting up once again with the same group from Camp Widjiwagan the next year, but this time in Wabakimi Park.

guys in the group would have this strong urge to overpower the leader. They'd try to fish better, paddle better, brew better coffee, constantly question my navigational skills, and even try to fart louder than me. But at the same time they were paying me for my skills and expertise. I just didn't get it.

Don't get me wrong here. I'm not knocking the male bonding type trip. I'm just not keen on guiding one. I've gone on plenty of those guy outings and had a positive experience, and it's evident that for both male and female groups spending time in the wilderness has value. To me, however, women in the wilderness have the ability to deconstruct gender and gender stereotyping. As Walter Ong said it, "All real women have more sense. Not all real men do. Masculinity has something futile about it." I like the attitude that women generally have on a trip. They don't push for mileage, traveling between two points as quickly as possible, but rather take in the pleasures of the social elements, a trip's ability to develop teamwork and lifelong relationships. They also seem to soak in their surroundings better, even appreciate nature more. Again, I'm not saying men do not exhibit the same value system; it just seems that when I guided them this was an afterthought rather than a priority of the trip.

The example of Don Starkell and Victoria Jason comes to mind. Starkell received instant fame after his 1980 canoe trip, paddling 12,000 miles from Winnipeg, Canada, to the mouth of the Amazon River. In 1991, Starkell joined forces with Victoria Jason in an attempt to kayak the Northwest Passage starting in Churchill, Manitoba, and concluding at Tuktoyaktuk, just North of Inuvik on the Beaufort Sea. Conflicts between them arose and the paddlers eventually went their separate ways. Starkell never made it to the finish line. He was in sight of Tuktoyaktuk but had to be rescued after being frozen in on the Arctic Coast, losing most of his fingers and some toes from frostbite. Jason, on the other hand, was successful and in her separate book — *Kabloona in the Yellow Kayak* — was harshly critical of Starkell's style of traveling. Jason claimed it was her common-sense caution and respect for the elements that enabled her to survive her journey unscathed, and it was Starkell using more brawn than brains that caused him to fail.

It's an interesting case study. But who's better — men or women — is not the point I'm trying to make here. It's that I find traveling in the wilderness with an all-woman group very satisfying. They remind me that time spent in the wilderness tends to allow people to feel complete, not divided. The women I guided were interested in being a part of nature, not conquerors over it. The female group experiences even enriched and complemented my male experiences and I became a better guide, and person, because of them.

A Few Adventurous Women

Isabella Bird: In 1873 she covered on horseback over 800 miles through the Rocky Mountains.

Grace Seton-Thompson: In 1900 wrote about her Rocky Mountain travels in her bestselling *A Woman Tenderfoot*.

Mina Hubbard: Was the wife of Leonidas Hubbard, who died of starvation in 1903 during a canoe trip from North West River to Ungava. Mina returned to Labrador two years later to complete the route herself.

Isobel Knowles: Wrote her account of a canoe trip down Quebec's Gatineau River in 1905 for *Cosmopolitan* magazine, highlighting the fact that she and her female partner successfully wore long skirts.

Esther Keyser: Became the first female guide for Canada's Algonquin Park (1927).

Connie Helmericks: Set out in 1965 on an Arctic canoeing trip with her two daughters, twelve and fourteen years old.

Cindy Ross: Hiked the 2,100-mile Appalachian Trail in 1979-80; more successful but less well known is her 1993 trek across the 3,100-mile Continental Trail with husband and two toddlers.

3

COOL CAMP GADGETS
AND
FASHION STATEMENTS

The tents weren't all that great, and I often slept under a canoe and would wrap my head in a towel to keep the bugs to a minimum.
— Esther Keyser, first female Algonquin park guide (1937)

I'M NOT EXACTLY WHAT YOU MIGHT CALL A GEAR HEAD. THOSE people who spend more time talking about their latest camp gadget than actually making use of it drive me insane. But that doesn't mean I don't like looking at the shiny and new. I hang out at outdoor shops during the off-season fingering all the new gear and can build a passion for a new product just as a child does for a toy in a store window a few days before Christmas. And I do, on occasion, treat an outdoors store like some kind of community center, spending time chatting with other obsessed campers about the best pick of gear for that particular year, but then ending up not buying anything.

I must confess that lately I've been spoiled when it comes to gadgetry. Over the past few years I've been doing a routine morning talk-show circuit showing the latest camp gear. Before the TV interviews I head to the local outdoor store to gather up the season's hottest items (and regretfully give them back when the tour is done) and then go live on air to discuss the pros and cons of everything from new mosquito repellent to solar radios. One item in particular, a urinary device enabling women to pee while standing up, was how the job all started for me.

Mike Walker models the latest in space-age fashion in Algonquin Park.

A camp chair is one of the top camp gadgets ... for campers over the age of forty.

I was being interviewed on a syndicated morning show for a recent book and decided to bring a few camp gadgets along to liven things up — including the plastic tube-shape fake penis contraption. The crew and female co-host had looked over the gear before the show and asked a few questions about the product, called Peemate. So they knew full well what the darn thing was. The main host didn't, however. He walked on set seconds before we went live. The guy acted more than a little arrogant and made some smart out-of-context remark about how silly camping was, and then grabbed the first gadget — which happened to be the female urinary device — and asked what it was. I'm not sure what prompted me, but live on television I said "It's a whistle; give it a try." He did. The crew and his not-so-arrogant female counterpart fell over laughing. The moment instantly became the joke of the century, at least in the world of morning shows, and almost every talk-show in the country phoned me the next day asking to be on their show to talk about my book — and the Peemate.

This fixation with new camp gear can't be healthy, at least for the pocket book. But it sure is fun trying out the stuff on trips. To me, camp gadgets are best defined as luxury items you can do without — but given the choice, you'd rather not. A camp chair, for example. Not just any camp chair, but one that allows you to sit high up off the cold, wet ground, equipped with a back rest and a cup holder. Now that's the life. A friend once brought a camp chair on our one-month canoe trip in Quetico Provincial Park. I teased him nonstop about packing such a bulky item along, that is, until he let me sit in it for five minutes a day. He instantly became my best buddy.

There's no sense fighting it. We've been trying to improve our comfort and take advantage of whatever's the latest in technology since we first went back to the wilderness. There are the rare campers who won't indulge and prefer the primitive lifestyle out there but I suspect they're the ones whose jobs are gadget-related and so they're desperate for an escape from the high-tech world. However, it is quite possible to get carried away. We've seen a few too many laptops glowing around fire rings recently. But if you follow the simple rule, "If you want to use it, then you carry it," things won't get too far out of hand. And if you don't want to carry it, then RV it at a campground and go hog wild. Over 90 percent of RV parks in North America have improved their facilities over the past couple of years to match the demand for high-tech gadgets. Most of the upgrading has been done to increase electrical amperage to the campsites themselves to handle things like phone, computer and TV hookups.

Eureka's new Hammock Tent — trees not included.

The top four categories major companies such as Bass Pro Shop, Mountain Equipment Co-op and L.L. Bean have been asked by their clients to improve are luxury tents, sleeping bags, camp chairs and cooking gear. You've got tents with built-in LED lights, down mummy bags that double as hooded parkas, collapsible camp rocking chairs, espresso kits, double-burner cookstoves and Titanium "sporks" (half spoon and half fork). Also big are the Eddie Bauer "Insta-bed" with a queen-size air mattress with simulated box springs, pop-up instant tents, and a bathroom tent complete with toilet and shower.

Experimental bug hat trip. None worked! Algonquin Park.

John Franklin's 1819 Equipment List
for his trip down the Coppermine River for 28 people

- a few unserviceable guns
- eight pistols
- 24 broad daggers
- two barrels of powder and balls for $\frac{2}{3}$ of that quantity
- nails and fastening for a boat
- some knives, chisels, files, axes, and a hand saw
- cloth and needles

- looking glasses
- blankets and beads
- two barrels of flour
- two cases of chocolate
- two canisters of tea
- 200 dried reindeer tongues
- portable soups
- arrowroot
- dried moose meat for ten days

HOMEGROWN GADGETS

My hobby of making my own camp gadgets started years ago when I had less money and more time on my hands. It started innocently enough with hand-sewed stuff sacks. I bought the material for 50 cents a yard and taught myself how to use my mother's heavy-duty sewing machine. Next was a reflector oven made of left-over aluminum siding and a makeshift wanigan produced by duct-taping two five-gallon buckets together.

It wasn't long before the military surplus store became my regular hangout, and to this day I still wear army fatigues and have a huge assortment of flannel shirts. My first cook set was a Salvation Army special, with household pots and pans that nest together; I knocked their handles off and handle them around the fire with an old pair of pliers.

Then there was my homemade fire starter phase, when I used a concoction of drier lint and sawdust mixed with melted paraffin wax and poured into a cardboard egg carton to make little fire-eggs. Plastic soda bottles substituted for Nalgene water bottles; heavy-duty garbage bags were used for pack liners and tent floor tarps; Tylenol bottles became match cases and freezer zip-lock bags served as map cases.

Eventually I reached the point where I could afford most of the important pieces of camp gear and stopped bothering to build my own. But old habits die hard and I continued with things such as placing a coffee filter in my water filter to extend the life of the replacement parts. I even cut up old blue-foam sleeping mattresses for knee pads in the canoe.

Now I build things more for a hobby, and if I had to choose the best overall homemade gadget I'd pick the beer can stove.

The beer can stove idea isn't new and if you've used or even seen a Trangia stove you'll notice the similarities. Dozens of homemade models are promoted on personal websites, made from everything from cat food cans to tomato paste containers. Soda or beer cans are more commonly used because of their bowl-shaped bottoms. Also, aluminum is an excellent thermal conductor, which helps in the vaporization of the fuel.

The basic design itself dates back over a 100 years. Before the Trangia stove, which has been marketed since the 1950s, there was 1904 design patented by J. Heinrichs of New York. A company called Safesport sold a stainless-steel version in the 1990s. But they all work on the same principle and are made of a double wall generator, a perforated burner ring, and an inner pre-heat chamber. The beer can model simply acts as a gas generator, moving heat from the flame to the fuel, which in turn enhances combustion and produces a very effective heat source. It's more than just a container that burns a liquid fuel. Having three separate parts creates a place for the fuel to be preheated and then a place for the vapor of the heated fuel to rise and burn off.

Beer Can Stove Directions

Step 1 DRINK 12 OZ. CAN OF BEER

Step 2 CUT OUT CENTER PIECE
• Cut out the large bowl-shaped center section of the can with a sharp utility knife. This process is easier if you keep a slight to moderate, not heavy, pressure on the knife as you continuously circle the bowl, scoring along the inside rim. Five to six rotations with the utility knife should be enough to remove the center.

• Another method is to drill a series of larger holes with a drill bit and cut the remaining aluminum between the holes.
• File rough edges with heavy-grade sandpaper

Step 3 MAKE YOUR HOLES
• Place the 12 oz. beer can upside down and on a hard surface.
• Using a push pin and small hammer (or very small drill bit), create 24 to 30 uniform holes around the outside ring of the can.
• The smaller the hole, the better, so try not to let the push pin penetrate all the way.

Step 4 CUT OFF TOP SECTION
• Evenly measure a ¾-inch (20 mm) circumference around the can below the punctured holes.
• Mark measurement with a permanent marker.
• Cut out section with a sharp utility knife, scissors or tin snips.
• File rough edges with heavy-grade sandpaper.

Step 5 DRINK 14.9 OZ. CAN OF BEER

Step 6 CUT BOTTOM SECTION
• Place 14.9 oz. can of beer upright and on a hard surface.
• Evenly measure a 1-inch (25 mm) circumference around the 14.9 oz. can of beer (the accuracy of the measurement is more important here than it is on the top section).
• Cut bottom section just as you did the top section of the 12 oz. can.

Step 7 MAKE INSIDE COMPARTMENT
• Cut a 1⅜-inch (35 mm) wide band off the remaining part of 14.9 oz beer can.
• Cut vertically straight through the middle to form a long, rectangular sheet of aluminum.
• Trim ends of rectangle so it measures 7½ inches (190 mm) long.

• Cut three small triangles on one elongated side of the rectangle (this will allow the alcohol fuel to flow from the center of the stove to the side walls).

- Cut a slit into each end of the rectangle ½ inch in and on opposite sides.
- Interlock the two slits to reform the circular band.
- You can also reform the rectangle to its original tube shape by overlapping the aluminum rectangle by ½ inch,

creating a smaller diameter cylinder, and holding the cylinder together with metal staples.

Step 8 STOVE ASSEMBLY

- Cut 6 to 8 vertical slits a quarter of the way up from the base up of the top beer can (the one with the pinholes in it).
- Place tube cylinder in the center of the bottom beer can.
- Insert the top beer can into the bottom (this is why the slits were cut).
- Place a strip of high temperature flue tape (or duct tape) over the slits and seam of the top and bottom cans.

Step 9 FUEL AND IGNITION

- Pour approximately 2 tablespoons of denatured alcohol into the center section of the lower can.
- Ignite fuel source. (A barbeque lighter might be a good idea.) Alcohol ignites quickly and has no visible flames in regular light conditions, so be careful!
- After a minute or so the ignited alcohol will heat up, achieving

an even burn temperature and a flame will exit the pinholes. A blue flame is desired; an orange flame means a lack of oxygen getting to the ignited fuel.
- If flames are not coming out of the pinholes, the inner tube is most likely too loose fitting.
- Take note that the stove can't be turned off; extinguish it with water if an emergency arises.

Step 10 POT STAND AND WINDSCREEN

- Your cooking pot must be held up about an inch from the flames. Rather than hold it there, try constructing a makeshift pot stand out of a wire hanger or use three or four metal tent pegs.
- A windscreen made of tin foil saves on fuel consumption.

It sounds confusing at first but once the beer is consumed and the stove is made, everything will become clear. And it's worth the effort. A beer can stove weighs in at 0.4 ounces (10 g) and will boil two cups of water in less than five minutes using 2 tablespoons of fuel.

The stove even outperforms some commercial butane or propane brands when in high-altitude or cold conditions where the gas is under less pressure. Fuel consumption isn't bad either, with heat output at 4800 BTU/hour or 1400 W). The fuel source itself (denatured alcohol) needs no special container for storage. They're pretty much silent, which is definitely not the case with such models as the Whisper Light Dragonfly. It's also a more environmentally friendly and sustainable fuel source than traditional gas, butane or propane.

It's true. A watched pot never boils.

UNDERSTANDING MY GPS MANUAL

I think, in a sense, it [GPS] transforms the wilderness surroundings into a television screen with coordinates on it. And I don't want that.

— George Luste, "The Tradition of Wilderness Travel," speaking at Canexus II, Peterborough, May 1996

Navigation in the wilderness has come a long way since Hansel and Gretel laid down a trail of breadcrumbs in the forest to find their way back home. With the introduction of the GPS (global positioning system), finding our way has progressed from fairy tale wisdom to Star Trek technology. The GPS has changed the way many adventurers travel by placing precise route-finding in the hands of the masses.

Global positioning systems are based on three elements: a network of satellites orbiting the earth that sends out electromagnetic frequencies (radio waves), control stations that track and control the satellites, and the GPS unit itself, which receives the satellite signal and calculates your position using latitude and longitude coordinates. Each satellite orbits the earth twice a day at a speed of more than 11,000 kilometers per hour.

GPS has been around since the late 1980s but has come a long way in recent years. First, the cost of a GPS receiver has dropped in half. You can pick up a half-decent model for between $100 and $200. The receiver itself is more accurate than ever. Problems with correcting for declination with a compass are a thing of the past. You can also enter map coordinates (latitude and longitude) and the receiver will provide a compass bearing, distance and time required to get to the desired location. And its best feature is that you can punch in your present position and save it as a waypoint, which should allow you to easily find your way back home, record a favorite campsite, or even mark a productive fishing hole. It can also help you figure out where to go, pointing you in the right direction just like a compass, when you enter virtual waypoints like a breadcrumb trail. On top of all that, a GPS lets you know how fast you are moving, how much distance to the next waypoint, and an estimated time of arrival.

Choosing a specific model becomes more difficult as the technology progresses. This year's model might be the latest and greatest but next year's will definitely beat it. However, even the simplest models have all you'll ever need. Just keep to the key features. Pick a multi-channel receiver (12 channels is standard) so you can lock on to a signal quicker (to save batteries) and if one satellite signal is blocked you can choose another. The average model will give you 12 to 15 hours of "navigation" time, which is all you would ever need (AA batteries are best since you are able to use rechargeable). Also, the more waypoints the unit can store, the better. A total of 200 is the norm but you might want to consider 500 or even 1000. Each waypoint represents a breadcrumb, and the more you have the easier it will be to find your way. And since the waypoints are identified by map coordinates, you'd better make sure your GPS is compatible with the area maps you're using.

Where a GPS becomes an excellent tool is when you want to quickly find a bearing to a given point or when triangulation is next to impossible to complete with a map and compass because of a lack of obvious landmarks. I finally bought one after guiding a family on a canoe trip in Ontario's French River delta system. Low water levels had dramatically altered what the topographical map showed and what we actually paddled past. I was looking for an inlet called Dead Island Channel and had to resort to asking a commercial fishing boat captain its position. We were drifting right through it at the time.

Quick History of Geocaching

Since the GPS was initially designed for military use, the U.S. Department of Defense started out by scrambling the signals to prevent enemies from pinpointing their targets. In 2000, however, President Clinton announced that the scrambling device would be turned off, allowing non-military types to increase their GPS's accuracy from 100 meters to a mere 15. Three days after the cancellation a computer consultant, Dave Ulmer, celebrated the demise of the scrambling system by hiding a bucket of goodies in a Portland, Oregon, forest and posted its position on a GPS users website forum.

From: Dave
Subject: GPS Stash Hunt... Stash #1 is there!
Newsgroups: sci.geo.satellite-nav
Date: 2000/05/03

Well, I did it, created the first stash hunt stash and here are the coordinates:

N 45 17.460
W122 24.800

Lots of goodies for the finders. Look for a black plastic bucket buried most of the way in the ground. Take some stuff, leave some stuff! Record it all in the log book. Have Fun!

Stash contains: Delorme Topo USA software, videos, books, food, money, and a slingshot!

The stash of goodies was found the next day. In the next few days more stashes were hidden in California, Kansas, and Illinois. A month later they were as far away as Australia. A web page for the worldwide phenomenon was established on May 8 by Mike Teague, who was the first person to find Ulmer's stash. On May 15 a mailing list was placed on Yahoo (then eGroups); and on May 30 the name "geocache" was coined by Matt Stum — replacing the original "Great American GPS Hunt"

Kinds of Geocaches

Cache-In Trash-Out: Geocachers meet and clean up trash in a given waypoint.

Night Cache: Same as a traditional geocache but done at night with reflector tape and flashlights.

Mystery Puzzle: First you must find information to locate the cache coordinates, which then lead to a waypoint containing a puzzle that must be solved to discover the coordinates.

Moving Cache: The finder of the geocache then becomes the hider, removing the item to another location and posting the new location.

Confluence Hunting: The cousin of geocaching, this was started in 1996 by Alex Jarrett, who wanted to find the waypoint of each land-based confluence in the world; a type of wilderness time capsule, according to GPS nerds.

That said, a GPS does not replace a good map and compass. First, if you do not know how to navigate with a map and compass, not only is it impossible to use a GPS properly, you also won't have a clue how to follow the instruction manual when you buy one. Basically, if you don't know how to navigate without a GPS, you'll be just as hopeless with one. They are not the "Salvation for Lost Souls" as some manufacturers have claimed.

Last season I received a phone call from a youth group leader in desperate search of a portage. It was after the dinner hour on a Friday night and he had just started guiding the kids on a nearby novice weekend route I had written up in a guidebook. I was more than dumbfounded that his first response was to call up the guy who wrote up the route and ask him where

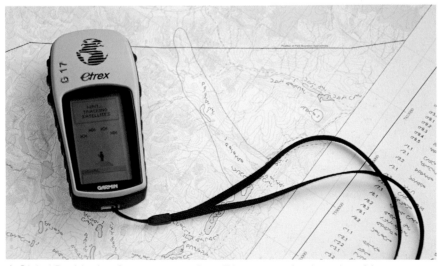

A Global Positioning System can make wilderness navigation a lot of fun — as long as you can understand the operator's manual.

the trail was rather than do a proper search himself. To be honest, I was so taken aback by the phone call that I refused to tell the guy where the trail was, bluntly suggested that he abandon the trip, and then hung up the phone. By morning, however, I was so guilt-ridden about my rude response that I drove up to the launch site and went for a paddle to see if I could find the group. And there, in the first bay of the lake, were five bewildered pre-teen boys and one goofball leader camped on a pint-size island.

Apparently they gave up the search just after 11 p.m. and I was all to blame for their mishap. When I approached the group, the leader told me their story and, unpacking his GPS, he went on in great detail about how his coordinates didn't match the bone-headed author's description. I then innocently suggested he stop scanning his new toy and simply look up from the screen to find the sign clearly marking the portage a few hundred feet away.

Yes, GPSs are fantastic tools for wilderness navigation. But nothing beats the skill of reading landmarks and thinking for yourself. After all, if Hansel and Gretel hadn't trusted their evil stepmother and used their intuition, they would never have found themselves lost in the first place.

GPS Alternatives

Sun Time
Using the sun is no more accurate than using the stars for figuring out direction; it's just much easier to travel during the day. Morning and evening are the easiest times to get a fix on direction since the sun always rises in the east and sets in the west. At high noon the sun is due south, but this can seem confusing. It is possible to locate south by using an analog watch equipped with an hour hand. With the watch in a horizontal position, point the hour hand toward the sun. The halfway mark between the hour hand and twelve o'clock is approximately south. If you have a digital watch, draw a clock on a piece of paper, marking the correct time, and follow the same instructions.

Homemade Sundial
It's possible to use the old "stick in the ground" method to tell direction. Plunge a stick into a flat piece of earth, away from any obstacles. Then, mark the point of the stick's shadow. Wait 10 minutes and mark the tip of the shadow again. Remembering that the sun travels from east to west, and that you are in the northern hemisphere, you know that north has to be between the two shadows, south is completely opposite, east is to the right of the original shadow, and west is to the left.

Reading the Stars
The easiest constellation to spot is the Big Dipper, which is the rump and tail of Ursa Major (The Great Bear). It's made up of seven bright stars, four in the shape of the bowl and three the handle. The bright star at the end of the handle of the Little Dipper (Ursa Minor) is the North Star, shining almost directly over "true" north. To use it for navigation it's best not to travel at night, for obvious reasons. Instead, mark the direction with a stick and wait until morning.

TRADITIONAL GEAR THAT STILL WORKS

I think we should talk about the mysterious values of this piece of leather (the tumpline) and the subsequent development of neck muscles that women find irresistible.

— Jim Spencer

There are times I embrace new technology and others when I revel in the traditional. There's not really a huge difference between the two. We're always coming up with new, lighter and more luxurious camping items and we always will. But what we call classic camp gear is simply gear that's been proven over time, and has become so commonplace there's no need to replace it with anything new or different. It's not that it has come back in style, as a retro-fad, but that it does the job time and time again.

The camp stove is a good example. It didn't take long for someone to come up with an alternative heat source to cook from instead of a finicky campfire. In 1881, Frans Wilhelm Lindqvist designed the first kerosene cook stove and sold it under the name Primus. It was originally just sold to friends and family but eventually the stove's popularity grew and it was mass-marketed by B.A. Hjort and Company (Bahco) as cheap, durable, smokeless and sootless. The device boiled water in less than four minutes.

Standard gear such as the camp stove has proven its worth time and time again.

The Optimus AB bought the rights to Bahco's Primus stove in the early 1960s. Even though models and fuel types may have changed somewhat since then, little has changed in the basic design.

The Swiss Army knife has changed little as well. In 1884 Carl Elsener invented a pocketknife that was approved by the Swiss Army and became an instant success. Thirteen years later Elsener patented another pocketknife that opened on both ends, containing six separate blades and requiring only two springs. Elsener called it the Officer's knife, but we know it today as the Swiss Army knife. In the early days of his company he narrowly avoided bankruptcy through the generosity of relatives and the knife itself never really became an official part of the army's equipment. Its popularity grew as officers in the Swiss Army began buying their own and soon Elsener was able to pay his relatives back the money owed. The Swiss cross has been on the handle since 1909, the same year Elsener's mother Victoria died, giving the company's brand name Victorinox. Over 34,000 Swiss Army knifes are produced annually, in 100 different variations — but all are based on the original patent.

In 1900 a salesman, W.C. Coleman, saw the potential of using a pressurized gasoline burning lamp instead of a normal coal oil lamp to light up a store window. He asked to market the product and bought the patent a year later. It was a slow start, but by 1914 he had improved on the lamp, making it so popular, especially in rural areas without electricity, that the U.S. government announced the Coleman lamp a necessary item. It still is today in campgrounds across North America.

Grumman canoes may have begun replacing wood and canvas models in 1945, but that doesn't mean they improved paddling abilities.

More Major Innovations in Outdoor Gear

1910 The zipper, first invented by Whitecomb I. Judson in 1893, is used on outdoor clothing and not long after on tents, packs and sleeping bags.

1912 Leon Leonwood Bean is the first to sew a waterproof rubber bottom sole to a leather-top boot and used the boot's popularity to start the L.L. Bean Co. The boot is taken on Admiral Donald B. MacMillan's 1923 Arctic expedition and the U.S. army used them during the Yom Kippur War. Almost 10 million have been sold.

1923 William C. Coleman introduces his first camp stove, a two-burner design that features a hot blast starter, eliminating the need for priming.

1925 Government surveys begin for the development of the National Topographic Mapping System.

1933 The Silva Company is established and produced the first navigational instrument that combines a compass and protractor.

1939 Nylon becomes a hot item, especially for making climbing rope, lightweight tents, packs and clothing.

1945 – The Grumman Aircraft Company replaces the traditional heavy wood and canvas canoe with a new lightweight model, constructed of aluminum.

1948 Velcro is invented, inspired from seed-burrs caught on wool socks.

1967 Lowe Company revolutionizes the use of internal frames for backpacks.

1968 Uniroyal begins the development of Royalex ABS plastic hulls for canoes.

1974 The first effective polyester synthetic insulation (Polarguard) is used for sleeping bags, replacing the old-style down-fill bags.

1975 North Face comes out with a lightweight geodesic dome tent, the first with flexible aluminum poles.

1975 Lifa polypropylene long underwear takes over classic cotton.

1976 W.L. Gore company introduces a new breathable rain-wear fabric called Gore-Tex.

1977 Therm-A-Rest mattresses begin relieving camper's bad backs across North America.

1980 Alex Tilley begins to sell his prototype sailing hat at Toronto outdoor shows.

1987 A bear repellent product called "Bear-Off" is invented by Ed Caesar, consisting of a red-pepper-based powder stored in a resealable plastic bag. The idea is to throw the powder in the face of the attacking bear, impairing its sense of smell and sight long enough for the victim to escape. Not long after, a spray repellant replaced the powder.

1994 Global Positioning System (GPS), first conceived by the USAF in 1960, becomes available for outdoor enthusiasts.

Eventually mold sets in, shoulder straps break, and the traditional canvas pack simply becomes a good prop for portaging photos.

Some canoeists call the canvas pack, more commonly known as the "Duluth pack," the most traditional canoe pack. Their claim is hard to beat. After all, its original patent dates as far back as 1882. Camille Poirer was a French-Canadian who traveled to Duluth, Minnesota, in 1870 and became a shoestore owner. In 1882 he filed for a patent for a packsack complete with a buckled flap, fancy leather shoulder straps, a conventional tumpline, a new-age sternum strap, and even an umbrella holder. Poirer sold the pack business to the Duluth Tent and Awning Co. in 1911, and they continued with the design, as well as canvas tents attached to cars, which became the first mobile homes. Woods Canada also produced a pack similar in style to the Duluth pack. Both styles haven't changed much since.

Another age-old packing device is the wanigan. The word, loosely translated, comes from the Native term for "kitchen," and many youth camps are devoted to it for that very reason. The wanigan makes an excellent storage bin for a large group's cookset. Basically, it's a wooden box, usually made of quarter-inch plywood (measuring 25 inches long, 12 inches wide, 15 inches deep) that's used to carry all the pots, pans, utensils and some food items. The lid makes a perfect cutting board and the box itself comes in handy for a serving table. It's a perfect system for keeping every-thing organized, eliminates shuffling through packs for last-minute items, protects breakables, fits snugly in the canoe, and will even float in the event of an upset. The portaging technique also makes good use of the tumpline, a system that's thought by many expert canoeists to be the only true way to carry a heavy load across the trail. You just place the tump on your head, making sure not to rest it directly on your forehead or too far back so that the weight wrenches your neck muscles. If only kitchen gadgets are stored in the box, it's usually light enough to even toss a small canvas pack on top as well.

The plastic olive barrel is today's waterproof version of a wanigan. In the mid-eighties a few canoeists began picking them up at yard sales and delicatessens in Quebec after realizing that the watertight containers were perfect for keeping gear dry, especially on river trips. Now you can pick them up at almost any outdoor store. Just like using the traditional wani-gan, however, it's a love and hate relationship. The barrel has all the advan-tages of the conventional wooden box — even having the lid do second duty as a cutting board — but in no way is the thing comfortable to carry. At least it doesn't rely exclusively on a tumpline system. The barrel also comes with shoulder straps or can be slipped inside a big canvas pack.

Plastic barrels are today's version of the wanigan.

The first dome-style tent was created after three friends — Murray Pletz, Jan Lewis and Skip Yowell — had their common A-frame tent ripped to shreds during a fierce storm in 1972. They went home, learned from their bad experience and formed a company called JanSport to produce a free-standing dome-shaped tent held together with three bendable intersecting poles.

The list of traditional or classic camp gear goes on, but I believe the point is proven, that many of the more popular items that have helped campers explore more wilderness areas are still doing the same today, with little change.

If your tent doesn't have good ventilation it will start smelling like the inside of a hockey bag just a few days into your trip.

GOOD FASHION SENSE

Contrary to what my wife tells people, the reason I like wearing my old wool sweater on camping trips is not because I'm too cheap to buy a new one. I wear it because it looks good on me. Yes, wool is also a sustainable material, perfect for dealing with changing weather conditions, and it sheds moisture. But the main reason I throw it in my pack is because I want to at least look as I have some fashion sense. I mean, really — as soon as those Michelin Man monster-sized down winter jackets went out of style, I made the switch to much more flattering high-tech outdoor wear. You too can be a sensible fashion icon. Today you definitely have lots to choose from.

Let's start with underwear. If you're thinking that outdoor skivvies are a private matter and have nothing to do with fashion (or ability to keep you cozy), think back to the union suit. That red cotton one-piece with a trap door was in vogue for years. Recently, however, what's replacing cotton undies is polypropylene (what was once known as polyester). The material has a two-layer system, with the outside fabric having a greater affinity for

Wool is still practical but fashionable in the north woods. Boris Swidersky, Killarney.

Bugs? What bugs? Shark Lake, Kawartha Highlands Park.

body moisture than the inside layer, which in turn pulls the sweat away from your body and lets it evaporate. The after effect is that you won't suffer from chills after building up a sweat and then stopping your workout. Wool is also used by some clothing manufacturers for the outside layer, which also soaks up the moisture and lets it evaporate. Odor used to be the main problem with polypropylene but new fabrics have silver or gold compounds incorporated in the fibers, which discourages bacteria from growing.

If you want to stay warm, the next layer, up top anyways, is usually either wool or fleece. Fleece technology has greatly improved since its inception. It's softer, compresses to a smaller size (remember those Cookie Monster jackets?) and gives more warmth with a much reduced weight. I prefer the shag look. It's a terrible choice for indoor carpets but for a fleece this texture has a low density but lots of room to capture air for insulation. There was a trend not long ago that pushed fleecy fabrics that shed wind and rain. They worked but your sweat had a hard time escaping, and most of the time you put on a waterproof outer layer to repel wind and rain anyway. Now more people are buying up fleeces that repel moisture from the inside, even if they lack good protection from the wind and rain. A hardshell fleece fabric used to make a soft-shell outer garment is the key here.

Warming Techniques

- Breathability is the key for keeping warm. If your inner and outer wear trap water vapor, you'll overheat too quickly, get trenched in your own sweat and soon get the chills.

- A windproof garment sounds good but keep in mind that if it prevents wind from penetrating then it also prevents sweat from escaping.

- Waterproofness is more important in warmer and really wet conditions but in cold winter conditions, especially during high-energy activities, breathability becomes more important.

- Stay away from cheap fleece. Low-budget material may look good but upon examination you'll find they are little more than heavy brushed polyester knits that provide poor insulation and eventually become matted and pretty much useless.

- Wearing less and dressing in layers keeps you warmer than one large coat.

- It's true that cotton kills. The small amount of insulation cotton has is quickly lost with the slightest moisture. Polyester is your best choice.

- Go baggy or go home. Tight-fitting garments, especially pants, might look nicer but there's little room for insulation and you'll get the chills quicker.

- No matter what you're wearing, the moment you start sweating you become dehydrated and will become cold and clammy. Pace yourself and try not to get a good sweat going if you can.

"At least the bugs aren't out." Alana tries to stay warm, Tatachikapika River, Ontario.

Pants are often an afterthought when it comes to both fashion and function. Too many people chose a thin pant and then wonder why they have cold feet. Leg insulation is critical for keeping up the body temperature. In the summer, try wearing a lightweight, tightly woven nylon pant that allows moderate wind resistance and a good amount of sweat to escape. In colder temperatures, a tightly woven fleece pant with a windproof and water-resistant layer works wonders. Just make sure the pants ride up high enough in the waist to keep the wind off your lower back but not so high that you look like a nerd.

Almost thirty years ago, Gore-Tex revolutionized outerwear fashion. It claimed to be the end-all fabric to block wind, shed water like a traditional rain jacket, and breathe out body moisture better than a wool sweater. But it didn't take long for hard-core outdoor enthusiasts to begin questioning the

Two hats are better than one. Ashley McBride, Kawartha Highlands Park.

claims being made. My first Gore-Tex purchase worked so badly that I actually went back to using a rubber rainsuit instead. Then came the era of soft-shell outerwear Gore-Tex. This worked 90 percent of the time but was still inadequate during a nasty rain storm. Nowadays the jackets have greatly improved but care still has to be taken when choosing which one to purchase for your type of outdoor sport. The lightweight Gore-Tex is good for all-around camping but when it comes to carrying a heavy pack through a brushed-over portage, you should opt for the heavier materials — or just buy a cheap rubber rainsuit instead and tell your friends you are going retro.

THE PERFECT CAMP HAT

I didn't give it much thought at first when my paddling buddy handed over his sleeping pad, rain jacket and canoe pack to his nephew. I just considered it a nice gesture; after all, we had finished our trip — 27 days paddling Quetico park — and his nephew was just beginning his — a summer spent working as a canoe guide for Scouts Northern Tier Camp. But when Andy handed over his canoe hat, a weathered Tilley complete with a sweat-stained rim and a dozen or so mosquitoes squashed on the cap, I definitely took notice. Giving away simple camp gear is one thing…but a canoe hat…that's like handing over your soul!

Wearing a hat on a canoe trip does much more than protect your bald spot from the ultraviolet rays or hide bad hair. A hat advertises your character out on a trip; it introduces your true self to passers by and announces to everyone that you're an individual, a true adventurer. And Andy didn't just wear a baseball cap; no, it was a preshrunk, water-repellent, full-brimmed Tilley. Not a fake Tilley, a true "tested through the intestine of an elephant" Tilley. My canoe partner is definitely not a fashion-designer canoe snob, but he knows a good hat when he sees it.

Maybe I'm more of a hat fan than Andy, but I just couldn't help but ask him all the way home why he would hand over his canoe bonnet, that special garment that protected his skull for 27 days in Quetico, not to mention on countless other trips in the north. I'm guessing that the taunting had some effect, because a week later he phoned up the camp to ask his nephew for the hat back.

That's when the bad news arrived. The nephew had misplaced it after lending it to a young Scout who was suffering from heat stroke. No one seemed to know where it was left behind.

Andy was okay with the mishap. I wasn't. I contacted the head camp counselor demanding they investigate poor Andy's lost hat. Throughout the summer a massive search went on, unknown to Andy, and it wasn't until the last week of the season that the hat was located, stuffed into the back corner of a bush plane docked somewhere north of Red Lake, Ontario. It was

Andy and his infamous Tilley hat. Quetico Park, Ontario.

immediately shipped to its rightful owner, with a long, drawn-out note of apology from a very sheepish nephew for being so callous.

So, what did Andy do? He decided to play a practical joke on the poor boy and replied to his nephew's letter, telling him "Thanks…but it's not my hat!" It took until the annual family gathering at Christmas for the joke to be let out of the bag, after Andy unwrapped a brand-new Tilley from a gift box handed over by his nephew. Thankfully, family members have a tendency to forgive and forget. His nephew just recently made the decision to work in the north again this season, and being the good Uncle Andy is, he mailed off some gear for him to borrow — including his new Tilley from Christmas, with his nephew's name inscribed inside.

GREEN GEAR

Living outdoors in any conditions can be done in comfort if you have the right equipment and attitude.
— Bill Mason, *Timeless Wilderness*

I once wrote an article for a magazine about the best rivers to paddle and made mention of one in western Canada that was endangered by the possible development of a gold mine. The next issue of the periodical revealed a strong letter of appeal from a lobbyist working for the gold mine. He claimed I was a "myopic dreamer" because most of the camp gear used today is made of all kinds of metals hauled out of the ground.

I have to admit that he had a point. Those of us who love spending time in the great outdoors feel a twinge of hypocrisy at times. We can have a negative effect on the environment too, from the places we go, the watercraft we use, the gear we pack, the clothing we wear and the vehicle we use to get there and back. However, we actually truly care about our ecological footprints, and are dedicated to lessening our impact as much as possible. These days there are products that work just as well and look just as good but cause less environmental damage. From hemp surfboards to recycled plastic underwear, we are bettering the planet one step at a time.

Clothing companies have recently seen the light. Ex Officio Tofutech Tee is made from a new fabric woven from stalks of soy plants to create a renewable, biodegradable and odor-resistant product. Fox River Bio Fiber Socks are 65-percent Ingeo fiber (polyester made from corn sugar) and are completely biodegradable. Blurr Alfa Pants provides a cozy and durable organic cotton climbing pant. Toray of Japan announced a waterproof/breathable shell that was free of Volatile Organic Compounds (VOCs) and other solvents. And there's even Icebreaker, who stayed real and used renewable New Zealand merino wool for a number of products.

Hats off to Patagonia for being the first to come up with a valid "green" product. They began way back in 1993 with a post-consumer-recycled polyester fleece. In 1996 they changed their entire line of outdoor wear to organically grown cotton. Now, together with Canada's Mountain Equipment Co-op, they've come out with 100-percent recycled polyester fiber-infused clothing. When you are done with your shirt, you mail it back to the company to be reused again as yarn in Japan.

PFDs (personal flotation devices) are becoming PVC-free. The manufacturing of polyvinyl chloride (vinyl) produces nasty carcinogenic and toxic pollutants that end up in water sources and the atmosphere. They even leach out onto the person wearing it. Now a foam that is PVC free is taking over the market. Mountain Equipment Co-op and Astral make a comfortable (and safe) PFD with an environmentally friendly filler.

The changes in footwear are also major but get little notice. Mion and Chaco, for example, use carbon-neutral materials as much as possible, and even provide a program where clientele can have their old sandals, shoes and boots resoled and restrapped. The glue used in resoling is made of a water-based, nontoxic substance, and you can even mail your old sandals back to the companies for them to send them off and be shredded and reused. Plus they run their factories on solar, geothermal or wind energy.

Going green when it comes to canoe and kayak manufacturing isn't as easy a task. Most products are made from molded plastics, fiberglass or Kevlar. Recycled plastics are thought to be the future but some major failures have occurred during production. Immersion Research hasn't changed their product much but they did install a biodiesel processor so employees can use the biofuel to run their diesel cars and/or heat their homes if so desired.

The list is endless. Tent companies such Millets One Earth are introducing organic cotton tents with tent poles produced with recycled aluminum or with less acid in the anodizing process. Thermo Pads are made from undyed bamboo fiber and filled with bamboo-based foam (the seal valve is even made of recycled aluminum). And there are countless electronic gadget companies (Brunton, Solio and more) that promote solar chargers

More Green Stuff

- Magnesium carbonate climbing chalk, also known as rock chalk, now comes in colors with natural pigments that match the tinge of the rock you're climbing to avoid that unsightly look.

- A device called the "Poop Tube" is available for climbers so they can go number two while dangling from a cliff.

- EBay offers Freecycle, a place on-line to take and give away secondhand outdoor gear and clothing.

- Ken Noguchi is slowly cleaning up Mount Everest. Five trips up the mountain have so far produced a pile of 9,000 kilos of the estimated 50 tonnes of rubbish left up there.

- Conservation Alliance encourages all outdoor businesses to help protect and conserve natural habitats.

- Mother's Day weekend has become the unofficial start-up date of the annual Wilderness Clean-up initiative, where volunteers maintain existing canoe routes by picking up trash and clearing out portages.

- Mo-Go-Gear makes camp stoves out of used beer cans and .22 magnum shells.

- Alcohol-based camp stoves can now be run on plant-based alcohol rather than petroleum-based fuel.

- Matunasco produces a surf wax made mostly out of organic ingredients.

- PETT Potable Environmental Toilet has developed a poop bag that's degradable and contains magical powder that transforms human feces into an odorless gel — now that's cool!

"Everything I'm wearing is made from totally recycled camp gear."
Rebecca Goostrey, Environmental and Sustainable Coordinator for
Mountain Equipment Co-op.

rather than the use of disposable batteries. Publications about outdoor sports
have come on line too. *Explore* magazine was the first to have 100-percent
post-consumer-recycled glossy paper and won the Aveda Environmental
Award for environmental leadership.

Being environmentally aware is tough. But it shouldn't keep you from
heading out there. Paddling a river, walking through a forest or climbing a
mountain are all activities more likely to convince you to be friendlier to
the earth. The more time spent in the outdoors the greater the sense of
stewardship — after that, all the other pieces seem to fall into place.

ALL THE THRILLS WITH NONE OF THE SPILLS

How We Get Around

I've learned that everyone wants to live on top of the mountain, but all the happiness and growth occurs while you're climbing it.

I LIVE IN PETERBOROUGH, ONTARIO — THE BIRTHPLACE OF THE modern-day canoe. This is a place that takes canoeing seriously, maybe too seriously. I remember coming to town twenty years ago with a new streamlined Kevlar canoe strapped to my truck. The local canoe club members nicknamed it the Potato Chip and suggested I don't show up for the next meeting until I had a *real* canoe.

What they meant of course was that I bring a cedar-canvas variety, preferably made a hundred years ago and refurbished or built with my own hands. And they were quite serious about me not bothering to return unless I had one. I've heard of cultural differences, but this was ridiculous. I came back for the next meeting, still with my Potato Chip, and I was instantly shunned.

Mind you, that was a long time ago and people change — but not in Peterborough. The last time I went to a canoe gathering in town, one man innocently asked if there were any kayak routes in the area. I've never seen a person ignored so efficiently.

I'm not knocking where I live. After all, I prefer canoeing to any other outdoor sport. So I'm quite happy there. But it seems if you're not born with

Have paddles, will travel. Family canoe trip, Temagami, Ontario.

a canoe paddle (or a hockey stick) in your hand in Peterborough, you're better off moving to another town. I'm sure other towns are not so different. There's probably a village of mountain bikers who shun backpackers or a community of kayakers who mock RV owners. There's also the debate over whether an ATV driver can get the same wilderness kick that a rock climber does. And there will always be new ways to transport yourself, and people who do a total switchover from one means to another due to a change in lifestyle or interests.

Combining all or some of these activities is, of course, quite acceptable — even normal. There's no law stating you can't canoe if you're a mountain biker or go backpacking if you usually kayak. You'll even look sportier hauling a canoe, bike or kayak atop your RV. Car-campers are also well known to mix it up, loading every possible piece of outdoor transport in their vehicle for their time out. The only difference is that the further into the wilderness you go, or the more solitude you seek out, the more complex it becomes.

Choosing a way to get there is one thing; packing the gear and having the expertise while you're there is another. It quickly becomes obvious that the means of transport greatly affects all the stuff you can take along with you and basically how long you can stay out. For example, canoeing on a lake near the campground is quite different from going on a multiday interior paddling trip; day hiking is nothing like going backpacking for a week or two. Statistics even show that the majority of kayakers are day-users only and that mountain bikers will spend the day in the woods and the evenings at the local pub. That's not to say all kayakers are lily-dippers and all mountain bikers are overly social. I know individuals who go on two-month kayak ventures and year-long bike treks.

The Next Best Outdoor Recreation

Recreational Tree Climbing: This is far beyond a child scrambling up a tree in the backyard. The new RCT sport is about the rush of going from cliff faces to tree trunks; and after making your way up a hundred feet or so, you camp for the night — without falling.

Parkour: This is the simple art of moving from point A to point B in the most proficient way one can think of, whether it's climbing over a wall or just jumping over it. The sport originated in French soldiers running obstacle courses and a guy named David Belle who started the craze back in the 1990s.

Riverboarding: The idea of maneuvering a body board around the rapids is quickly becoming as popular as whitewater kayaking. Why? Because it's easier.

Paddleboarding: Reinvented by surfing guru Laird Hamilton, the act of standing on top an elongated surf board and propelling yourself with an outrigger paddle is a huge hit for people looking for fun in small waves and a chance to do a good workout.

What's more important than what you use to get you around while camping is that you actually go camping. We're all basically looking for the same thing, and we are more alike than you think — although with slight differences in character to make things interesting. So, whether you choose to canoe or kayak open water or bike or hike a trail shouldn't really matter as much as simply getting out there to do it.

Actually getting out into nature is far more important than how you get there. You have to look way up to see the tops of the old-growth pine in Quetico Park.

"If only the canoe I portage was this light." Author Kevin Callan discovers his daughter's new Barbie camping accessory.

MR. CANOEHEAD

My passion for canoeing began at the age of twelve. My father and I were at a remote fishing lodge in Algoma, Ontario, and spent a good part of the week trolling the main lake without much luck. The second-last day, we decided to borrow one of the lodge's beat-up aluminum canoes and portaged into a neighboring lake to try for speckled trout. We caught plenty of fish, but it was the idea of the canoe itself taking me to such a special place, a place that truly characterized remote wilderness, that hooked me. I've yet to look back. At the age of 44, I've never had a full-time job; and the jobs I have worked at all had something to do with paddling wilderness areas. It's a dream come true.

The canoe is still my choice for getting around out there. It's the one thing that binds me irrevocably to the wilderness. I even find the motion of paddling the craft itself very methodic; the action of drifting across a calm lake or being pulled downriver is very Zen-like.

My passion may have something to do with the fact that I'm Canadian as well. Even though canoeists owe a great deal to Scottish philanthropist John MacGregor, who in 1865 popularized canoeing as a recreational sport across Europe and the United States, I doubt few would argue with the claim that the Canadian identity itself lies with the canoe. If Canadian film producers ever wanted to depict the opening of Canada's wilderness the way Hollywood characterized winning the Wild West, the hero wouldn't be straddling a horse, but rather crouched down in a canoe, paddling off into the sunset. The packsack, paddle and portage are as much pioneer icons as the chuckwagon, boot spur and ten-gallon hat. Maybe the closest this aspect of Canadian culture has come to be represented in film (the work of Bill Mason excluded) is in the Frantics' Mr. Canoehead, a superhero who had his head inadvertently welded to his aluminum canoe by a stray lightning bolt.

When I spot a car barreling down the highway with a canoe strapped to its roof, I don't see a somewhat inexpensive recreational watercraft owned by some poor fool who can't afford a speedboat; I see a way of life.

I also like the people who paddle, and there was a moment this past summer that I rediscovered that idea. It all happened on a canoe trip with my wife and daughter. I like to keep a relaxed pace when I trip, but that afternoon Alana (and our dog, Bailey) and I couldn't get our dawdling daughter through the portage quickly enough. A curious black bear seemed as interested in us as I was in it, and to add to the anxiety a column of storm clouds was collecting upwind.

Our push-off from the portage was hasty. It wasn't until we were halfway around the lake, losing ground to the storm, that I discovered our spare paddle was missing. I knew exactly where I had left it — tucked into the marsh grass in the muck that sucked at our boots as we hurried into the canoe — but I wasn't going back. Alana and I had our two-year-old daughter with us, and you have a maximum of an hour-and-a-half of grace time

Paddling Basswood Lake, which borders Boundary Waters in United States and Quetico in Canada.

while paddling with a two-year-old. We were already in too deep. Besides, the storm would soon be on us, and the bear was probably licking his lips in a carefully selected ambush spot near the paddle. So I left it.

Alana questioned the decision, but I assured her I would put out a request for the paddle on some canoe website chat forums. I remember being surprised she thought that would work. It took me a while to post the message, but I received a response the very day the notice went up. A maintenance crew had found my paddle and handed it over to an outfitter.

After a moment of marveling at how honest, close-knit and web-addicted canoeists are, I called the outfitter. He told me he had been handing it out to clients to use as a spare paddle. I had to wait for the last group to come back before I could retrieve it.

I admit I was worried to hear my paddle was being abused by other canoeists. But then he listed the trippers who had used the paddle already: a mother on her first trip with her two teenage daughters, environmentalists campaigning to save a stand of old-growth forest and a solo paddler trying to escape reality. That's when I saw the bigger picture. I may have lost a paddle but I had found a way to gain a wider perspective on the reasons people take paddle in hand to canoe.

To me the stories of why the canoeists ventured into the wilderness were more valuable than a spare blade. In the end, I told the outfitter to keep handing out my paddle to his clients, but only if he would report back to me about the paddlers who had used it and why. Who knows what will come of it: a book idea, an immensely lucrative magazine article, or just enough positive energy from other paddlers to remind me to paddle as much as I can — spare paddle or not.

> August is laughing across the sky
> Laughing while paddle, canoe and I,
> Drift, drift,
> Where the hills uplift
> On either side of the current swift.
>
> Be strong, O paddle!
> Be brave, canoe!
> The reckless waves
> you must plunge into.
> Reel, reel.
> On your trembling keel,
> But never a fear my craft will feel.
>
> "The Song My Paddle Sings," E. Pauline Johnson

The Canadian Stroke

How do you paddle a canoe in a straight line? You can power forward and then change sides every time the boat begins to veer slightly away from your paddling side. But unless you have a bent-shaft paddle, this is considered the most amateur technique in the paddling community and will get you laughed off the water in no time. You can twist the paddle blade toward the canoe after completing each forward stroke, treating the paddle somewhat like a ship's rudder. But this is known as the "goony stroke," and for good reason; every time you twist inward you put on the brakes. Then there is the J-stroke, which is the ultimate steering stroke. You twist the paddle outward to form the letter J, which forces the canoe back on course while still keeping your forward momentum.

The definitive steering stroke for canoe trippers, however, is the Canadian stroke. It was actually the Americans who came up with the name (originally it was called the knifing J-stroke). A well-executed Canadian stroke is the pinnacle of perfection in motion, a skill that comes only after extensive canoe tripping. It starts off the same as the J-stroke, but instead of pulling the blade abruptly out of the water after the J is complete, the paddle is "knifed" forward under the surface of the water until about halfway through the recovery. This saves both time and energy since you have to place the paddle forward for the next stroke anyway. The power face of the paddle faces the sky and the main trick is to get the proper angle while the blade is being pulled forward through the water. Too much and the paddle will burst out of the water and too little and it will dive deep below the surface like a submarine. The pressure applied to the paddle while it is being pulled up through the water and the length of the time it's kept below the surface is what determines how much the canoe veers back the other way.

To master the stroke it takes a lesson or two, or about a week of canoe tripping (in Canada, of course) will suffice.

The Canadian stroke is the definitive steering stroke for canoe trippers.

The biggest advantage of the kayak is it gives you the ability to go out on your own and propel yourself according to your own skill level.

KAYAKING

It all started when I was asked to be involved in a friendly debate on live radio about what was better — canoeing or kayaking. I was the canoeist and the manager of a kayak store was the opposition. I think we both made valid points but in the end the kayaker won. It was plain arrogance that made me lose the discussion. I kept trying to dissect the similarities between the two watersports and the kayaker kept proving they were the same. There's not much difference between the two vessels, and there's not much difference between the people who paddle them.

It's also true a kayak is basically made for big, expansive water. With a lower profile (and a sealed top deck) the kayak stays much drier, making it less easily influenced by crosswinds and far more navigable on large, choppy bodies of water. A kayak is narrower than a canoe but feels more stable. There's also less boat to push through the water, which mean less effort is required to produce more speed. Probably the most important element, however, is the advantage of being on your own, propelling yourself according to your own skill level but still able to enjoy the company of others while out on a trip. One of the biggest skills required for tandem canoeists is communications between one another. Time on the water can soon become extremely stressful if you're not getting along with the other person sharing the canoe with you. You could go solo in a canoe, of course. But the perception of solo canoeing is that it takes far too much skill to master. There are two-seated kayaks, but they've been given the nickname "divorce boats" by the paddling community.

As a consequence of losing the debate, I thought it would be fair for me to head out on a kayak trip to see what all the fuss was really about. I chose to circumnavigate Philip Edward Island in the northeast corner of Georgian Bay, Ontario. It's been rated by at least half-a-dozen outdoor magazines as one of the top ten places to kayak in North America.

I'm glad no one was around to witness me loading up at the put-in. I looked like a complete dork. It took me three attempts to find room to stuff all my gear under the deck (my skirt was on backwards), and I went for an unintentional swim while trying to enter to cockpit. It's not as if I was going about it blind: over the three previous weekends I had completed a full introductory course in paddling a kayak. But it was all still very new to me, and I was a little nervous. For almost 30 years I had used a canoe to travel across the water. Loading up and pushing off from shore in an open boat was nothing out of the ordinary. But this just wasn't the same thing, and it was darn embarrassing for a seasoned canoeist. And being such a canoe-head, I still wore my regular uniform of plaid shirt and baseball cap rather than get decked out in full Neoprene ensemble.

I started to settle down a bit while paddling around the river outlet at the put-in, and spent a few minutes going over my paddle strokes and even

There are two-seated kayaks, but they've been given the nickname "divorce boats."

practicing a self-rescue. No one was there to witness it, but it was a textbook recovery. I was quite proud of myself.

After that, I figured I was ready for the big stuff and convinced myself to exit the protective cove. And there to greet me was a continuous line of large surfing waves. The chop wasn't huge, but it was impressive enough that had I been in a canoe I would have definitely turned tail and returned to the put-in. It was surprising, but what actually encouraged me to move forward was the thrill of paddling the big water into the vastness of Georgian Bay. There's a fine line between feeling thrilled and feeling anxious, even a little nauseous, but the more my double-bladed paddle propelled me through the troughs the more I liked being there, and the more I realized why the kayaker had won our debate. She had spent time emphasizing the wild surroundings a kayak can introduce to you; I was too busy making points about design and flexibility of the canoe.

Like the canoe, kayaking is a passion that grows slowly. But the more you paddle a kayak, the more the boundlessness of sky and water will summon you. I went kayaking again, and then again. I fell in love with the huge horizons, or no horizons at all. There's absolute beauty where sky and water merge. On one trip I navigated through thick fog, with just the faint sounds of the surf to tell me that the shoreline was nearby. I pushed through massive

Mastering an Eskimo Roll

Kayakers come in two character types: newbies who capsize and flail around until they pop out of their skirt and swim to the surface and the elitists who perform an Eskimo roll and continue on before anyone notices they flipped.

It's true that if you're playing in serious rapids in one of those mini playboat kayaks, knowing how to recover after flipping over like a turtle is mandatory. It's not, however, if you're paddling a sea kayak in open water (getting your boat righted by another paddler can suffice). Completing the roll is just plain cool, though. There's nothing better, or more convenient, than to upright yourself seconds after capsizing — and it's even more gratifying if you're paddling with others who would mock you.

Before heading out to give it a try, keep in mind that rolling has little to do with strength. It's more of an exercise in control and balance, where you must believe in proper technique if you want to pop back up to the surface. And to learn proper technique you need to take a course. Very few kayakers have successfully mastered an Eskimo roll without taking a course.

You will learn that what happens under the water is more important than what happens on the surface. Think like a duck. The real trick, however, is to fight the urge to bring your head up from the depths first. A proper roll has your head coming up last. I know that action goes against instinct, and that breathing air is likely your priority, but if you come up for air before the maneuver is complete down below, then the jig is up for sure.

swells, low-bracing and combating seasickness throughout the day, but loving every minute of it. I felt alive. It was clear that I was in love with my surroundings, a very natural landscape that would never have been so clearly introduced to me if it wasn't for the kayak. Yes, I've had similar experiences in a canoe, and the only real difference with the kayak was the ability to paddle big water, plus the fact that I didn't have to be stuck in a confined space with a paddling partner I didn't necessarily like. With a kayak I could travel with a group and experience the wonder of it all, or just as easily be alone to soak in the beauty. With points such as these, no wonder the kayaker won the debate — now, if I can only get her to try a canoe.

CAR-CAMPING

Along with milk and vegetables kids need a steady diet of rocks and worms.

My parents introduced me to camping by sleeping in a tent, which was beside another tent, which was beside yet another tent. We then moved on to a tent-trailer, which was beside another tent-trailer. You get the idea. My dad's dream was to own a better class RV, the one that's a step closer to a mobile home. And I remember having great times, playing at the beach all day and meeting new friends. I eventually moved away from the world of RVs and now much prefer to camp in the remote wilderness, where there's no snoring neighbor who owns a yappy dog and a dozen unruly kids.

Camping in a private or public campground, what some like to call "car-camping," certainly has some disadvantages. However, I wouldn't pass on the experience growing up and certainly haven't completely stopped camping beside others in tents and trailers. I quite enjoy the lifestyle; it's a type of outdoor recreation that offers great deals of comfort, convenience and flexibility. Some people choose car-camping over cottaging because it takes them to different locations every year; others choose it because they can return to the same familiar campground, campsite and campmates year after year.

Today's RVs are far more luxurious than anything my parents ever owned. While traveling north last year I stayed at a government campground and ran into some old friends who owned the biggest rig around. It was loaded with all the modern amenities: shower, central air conditioning, propane heating, oven, side-by-side refrigerator/freezer, big-screen television with surround-sound CD and DVD player, video game system, stereo, well-stocked bar and wine rack, GPS unit and closed-circuit rear-view cameras for helping back the monstrosity between trees and rocks. I was camped beside them, equipped with a single pup-tent, sleeping bag, and a six-pack of beer stored in a cooler bag. After enjoying some refreshment at their campfire I ended up sleeping in their spare bedroom rather than crawling into my miniature dog house next door.

I had a great evening but I must admit that I first found the visit overwhelming, especially because I had just finished camping in the interior section of the park and was just using the campground as a way to freshen up before heading for home. I was mostly taken aback by watching their kids gather around with friends and socialize over video games and movies around the fire rather than toasting marshmallows or playing endless games of Scrabble. But I thought about it, and came to the conclusion that those kids represented me as a child (minus the video games and movies, I guess). And now look at me. I travel extreme remote wilderness areas with a passion. These young campers were just getting their first taste of a home away from home.

Who's to say that car-camping today doesn't match up to my experiences I had as a child? Last year over 9 million RVs were roaming the highways of North America. The popularity of the sport has boomed, with a more than 20 percent gain in the past year or so, which is astonishing considering record-high gasoline prices. Over 370,000 units were shipped to new customers in 2008. New studies also show that 94 percent of parents and grandparents who RV with their children or grandchildren overwhelmingly consider it the best way to camp with kids, and the best way to foster a love for the outdoors. Who can argue with that statistic?

Car-camping comes with all the comforts.

What's an RV?

RVs fall under two main categories — towables and motorhomes. A towable is what's towed by your car or light truck, unhitched and left at the campsite (and yes, it's illegal to travel in them while they are in motion).

- **Camp Trailer:** The folding camp trailer (the simplest and least expensive, at $5,000 to $10,000), is basically a tent pitched on wheels with some cool amenities inside such as bunks, a stove and a small fold-out dining table.

- **Teardrop Trailer:** This model, taking its name from a streamline shape, was popular in the 1930s and 40s and is now seeing a moderate resurgence. It's lightweight, easy on gas, moderately priced ($5,000 to $12,000) and has kind of a retro fun to it.

- **Truck Camper:** The next step up is a tent-like box structure mounted on the back of a large-scale pickup truck ($5,000 to $20,000). Sportsmen seem to love them and they come equipped with a sleeping area, stove, dining area and stereo that continuously plays country and western music.

- **Travel Trailer:** Lots of designs for this model and a range of lengths from 10 to 35 feet long ($8,000 to $80,000). Some can be extended widthwise by slide-outs and many have tops that can be lowered while being towed or stored. Most can be towed by a regular car or truck.

- **Fifth Wheel Travel Trailer:** Similar to travel trailers except for a cab-over attaching to the hitch area and multiple slide-outs ($10,000 to $120,000). All designs are luxurious and considered by some owners as livable as motorhomes.

- **Motorized RV (Motorhome):** You can go pee, snack, or watch TV while the trailer is in motion. But most owners end up hauling a small car behind them to travel about after setting up at the campground.

MOUNTAIN BIKING

"Men should never ride bicycles. Riding should be banned and outlawed. It is the most irrational form of exercise I could ever bring to discussion." So says Dr. Irwin Goldstein, expert on infertility in men.

I lost a canoe companion to the sport of mountain biking. He used to go on all kinds of paddling trips until he bought padded bike shorts, a streamlined helmet and a bicycle that cost more than my fleet of canoes combined. Now he's hooked and hasn't joined me on a canoe trip in years. I don't necessarily miss him. And I don't necessarily hold any grudges either. Mountain biking is really cool.

I spend lots of spare time mountain biking myself. But I'm not as fanatical about as my former canoe-mate. He compares mountain biking to downhill skiing; come to think about it, he's a downhill ski nut as well. (Instead, I spend the winter cross-country skiing.) He lives for the moment of going downhill on a mountain bike really fast. It's a moment in time when skill and experience is telling you don't do it, you're not in control, but the endorphin kick tells you to give it a try anyway. It's not as if other sports don't give the same sensation as mountain biking, but there's definitely something to be said about high speeding down a mountain slope, banking through a tight corner, shifting gears on an open stretch and then pushing up another hill to do it all over again.

But I'm a sissy when it comes to downhill racing, using the brake way too often because I know how much it's going to hurt when I fall off. As with cross-country skiing, I'd rather bike at a pace that allows gawking at things along the trail as I ride by. Mountain biking brings me back to childhood days of riding a bike around town. I took my bike everywhere when I was a kid. I rode to school, rode to my first job, rode every Saturday morning to my favorite trout stream, and rode to pick up my very first date (which was a stupid idea, by the way). My bicycle gave me my first feeling of independence. When you're too young to have a driver's license, it gives you an amazing sense of freedom. That's truly the only reason I would agree to adorn myself in sausage-squeezing, reveal-it-all bike shorts.

My bike back then wasn't a real mountain bike, though. Legend has it that the true mountain bike came out of California in the mid-1970s when a group of road racers headed off to check out Mount Tamalpais with single-speed Schwinn cruisers equipped with balloon tires. The group, calling

How to Fix a Flat Tire in 10 Easy Steps

1. Remove the wheel with the flat from the bike.

2. Pry the tire off the wheel rim on one side of the wheel. You may need to use a tire iron or something similar to get it started and slide the tool down the rim to remove the wheel (fatter mountain bike tires are easier to remove than road racing bike tires).

3. Once you've taken off the entire side of the wheel, pull out the tube from beneath the wheel.

4. Locate the puncture in the tube by blowing it up with a pump and watching for where the air is being released from, and then patch it or replace the entire tube. It's also a good idea to mark the position of the valve so once you find the puncture you can match up that area on the wheel to see if whatever caused it is still in the tire.

5. Pump a little air into the tube and reinstall it under the wheel.

6. Stick the valve through the valve hole.

7. Work the lip of the tire on one side back into the wheel rim with your fingers (you may need the tire rim to use as leverage for the last part), and then do the other side.

8. Reattach the tire to the bike.

9. Pump up the tire and then release the air to let out any kinks that may have formed between the tube and wheel.

10. Pump the tire back up again.

A bicycle gives you ultimate independence.

themselves the Morrow Dirt Riders, then re-outfitted their bikes with back and front drum brakes and motorcycle levers. Other racers were inspired, including Joe Breeze, who in 1977 constructed the Breezer, and Gary Fisher, Charlie Kelly and Tom Ritchey, who two years later marketed the first bike frame under the company name MountainBikes.

Where's my canoe buddy now? Well, he's a downhill ski instructor and president of the local mountain bike club. I last saw him on an expensive carbon-fiber racer, wearing multi-color spandex shorts and a hunter-orange lighter-than-air helmet. His wife-to-be was wearing white shorts and white helmet — which was fitting since it was their wedding day. The couple had met while mountain biking and decided to hold the ceremony on their favorite riding trail. Thankfully I wasn't in the wedding party since my bike is owned by my wife, and so are my bike shorts. Standing beside the happy couple would have been a tad embarrassing.

Hiking through a forest is a great way to absorb the intrinsic values of nature.

WALKING IN THE WOODS

Walking is man's best medicine.
— Hippocrates, the Father of Medicine, 460–377 B.C.

Even though I consider myself a regular canoehead, and would therefore characterize a hiking trail as the longest portage ever created, I still like walking through the woods. I grew up reading Colin Fletcher and Chris Townsend. Bill Bryson's *A Walk in the Woods* has to be one of my favorite books. Reading aside, walking with a pack on still hurts a lot more than paddling. My first real hike, lasting ten days and measuring over a hundred kilometers, did my knees in for the year, I lost three layers of skin off my soles, and I dropped almost 10 pounds. My body eventually recovered, I got back on the horse, as they say, and walked the Lake Superior Coastal Trail, and then injured myself even more. I went out a third time, basically because a woman I was dating at the time preferred hiking over canoeing, and I liked her enough to hide my agony. That woman became my wife, and as a tradeoff for all the canoeing we now do together, I agree each season to do one major walk in the woods.

The motivation for most people, including me, is that walking is our most fundamental means of getting around. In fact, the act of how we walk even separates us from all other species. It's also one of the biggest unanswered questions humans have; why did we start walking upright in the first place? Biologists and anthropologists have endless theories, none of which are concrete enough to satisfy anyone. Charles Darwin proposed it allowed us to have two limbs free to use tools. Other theorists believe our tree-living ancestors walked two-legged along branches, using their arms for balance. Some even claim it was so the male of the species could show off their genitals and either frighten off rival males or attract interested females. A new study even claims that humans walk on two legs to reduce energy costs and that chimpanzees "knuckle-walking" are three times less efficient.

A much bigger question, however, is not how we walk but what why. What do we get out of the act hiking itself? After all, it's our slowest means of travel.

For me, taking a walk through the forest is the best way to absorb the intrinsic values of nature. Some noted philosophers used walking to get their thoughts going. Jesus Christ wandered the wilderness for 40 days to deal with the temptations of the devil. Wilderness visionaries such as John

Bill Bryson said it best when he gave his reason for walking the Appalachian Trail with his buddy Katz. It was because a little voice in his head said "Sounds neat! Let's do it!"

Muir and Henry David Thoreau walked a great distance to experience the wilderness landscape. (Muir walked for two months in 1868, from San Francisco to Yosemite, and Thoreau walked a hundred days in 1866, from Montreal to Quebec City.) But you don't need a major pilgrimage to become familiar with nature. You just need to travel by your own means, on foot, to feel connected.

The flip side of all this, of course, is that we no longer walk as far on a regular basis as people did back in Muir, Thoreau or Christ's time. The automobile has spoiled us. We walk on average 350 meters a day, according to Bill Bryson. We think nothing of driving an hour out-of-town to a super-size

North America's Big Hikes

- **Appalachian Trail:** A total distance of approximately 2,200 miles (3,540 km) and extends through the states of Maine, New Hampshire, Vermont, Massachusetts, Connecticut, New York, Pennsylvania, Maryland, West Virginia, Tennessee, North Carolina and Georgia.

- **Pacific Crest Trail:** Runs through three western states of California, Oregon and Washington, measures 2,650 miles (4,260 km), and is rated one of the most popular long hikes in the United States with thousands of users per year.

- **John Muir Trail:** The trail measures only 211 miles (340 km) but it's a classic walk that should be done by the wilderness treks history buff. Set in the Sierra Nevada mountain range of California, it joins the longer Pacific Crest Trail — the same trek Muir once took — and was built a year after his death in 1915.

- **Continental Divide Trail:** This 3,100-mile (4,990 km) trek goes from Mexico to Canada, passing through five western states, Montana, Idaho, Wyoming, Colorado and New Mexico.

- **Trans-Canada Trail:** A coast-to-coast trail that's still being built, measuring 10,000 miles (18,000 km) in length, from Saint John's, Newfoundland, to Victoria, British Columbia.

- **The Bruce Trail:** This 500-mile (800 km) trail stretches across southern Ontario's Niagara Escarpment, is walked by over 400,000 hikers a year, and is the oldest hiking trail in Canada (opened in 1967).

- **West Coast Trail:** Only 47 miles (75 km) long, this is not by any means a long trail but it's rated one of the toughest in North America. The route, on British Columbia's Vancouver Island (Pacific Rim National Park), goes from Bamfield to Port Renfrew, and is definitely not for the faint of heart.

- **Y2Y Trail:** This trail is still in progress and remains more a vision to connect wildlife corridors between Yellowstone (west-central Wyoming) and the Yukon (Peel River) than an actual trail. The 1,990-mile (3,200 km) distance was first walked by Jim Stoltz between 1997 and 2002 but its popularity grew more after Karsten Heuer wrote about his 1998-1999 trek in his book *Walking the Big Wind.*

A walk in the woods can be one of the most effective stress relievers.

shopping mall to catch a sale but won't even consider taking a stroll to the corner store to buy necessities such as bread and milk. Of the 3,000 hikers a year who attempt to walk the entire Appalachian Trail from Virginia to Maine, only about 300 make the entire distance. We're definitely getting lazier.

On the other hand, however, hiking is still rated the top outdoor recreational sport in North America. After all, a hike in the woods, even if it is 350 meters, is much more glamorous than a walk to the corner store. A hike frees the soul and, according to Bryson, "You exist in a tranquil tedium, serenely beyond the reach of exasperation." It's a time of mental, spiritual and physical rejuvenation. If you think about it, going for a walk may no longer be the main way we're mobile each and every day but it has increasingly become the way we deal with the stress of day-to-day life.

If you are having an argument with your spouse, then go for walk; pondering a new career move, go for walk; having trouble with your teenage daughter or son, go for a walk; questioning your faith, go for a walk; being tempted by the devil, go for a walk. It's what we do to contemplate life, a way to simplify things so we can do nothing else except think.

5

FEELING AT HOME IN THE WILDERNESS

Some trails are happy ones,
Others are blue.
It's the way you ride the trail that counts,
Here's a happy one for you.

— "Happy Trails," Dale Evans Rogers

COMFORT ON A CAMPING TRIP CANNOT BE OVERRATED. After years of spending as much time as possible outside, I have to say that anyone who still believes in the old idea of just surviving your time in the woods hasn't a clue what the joy of camping is all about. Do yourself a favor and make sure it's a pleasurable experience, as much as you can, at least. Those individuals who insist on "roughing it" tend to go once or twice in their lifetime, check "camping" off their to-do list, and then move on to other sports. But if you're a dedicated camper, or a novice who wants to commit to spending time outdoors, make yourself as cozy as possible and then you can look forward to a lifetime of blissful experiences.

However, I am also the first to agree that being comfortable while camping out isn't easy at times. Remember the story of the princess and the pea? Well, camping is no fairy tale. Imagine if she had to hike up a mountain side or take on a mud-caked portage first, then try to sleep on that darn pea.

It took me a few years to figure this pea thing out. In fact, it was the year I turned forty. It seemed every part of my body hurt at the end of a day on the trail. In my youth I would just tell myself to tough it out or laugh it off

"A shot of rum and you're allowed in." Scott Roberts collects a toll for entry into the Eureka bug shelter.

with the others I shared the pain with. "Bring it on," I'd yell. I'd even act as if it wasn't a real trip unless I felt pain. My change in attitude came simply from growing older and, well, growing up.

My body just doesn't bounce back like it used to. "Roughing it" has lost its appeal. Yes, I'll tough it out if and when I have to, as long as I have a good supply of painkillers. I've been on enough bad trips that I know there's a pot of gold at the end of the rainbow. But I'll also try desperately to avoid the hurt. I pack a camp chair, have a cozy sleeping pad, fluffy goose-down sleeping bag and as much high-tech gear as I can "comfortably" fit in my pack. Remember, the princess' worth was proved because she felt the pea under the twenty mattresses and twenty eiderdown feather beds. In fact, she turned black and blue because of it. The fairy tale had nothing to do with her pain threshold but more with her ability to be realistic. So be real and camp comfortably.

THE BIRTH OF THE THERM-A-REST

It's odd that it took so long to go from sleeping on tree boughs to reclining on high-tech mini air mattresses with goose down floating around inside to keep you toasty warm at night. After all, a desire for comfort has always been the impetus for camp inventions and there's always been a strong desire to have a comfortable sleep.

Traditional "how to" and scouting books gave detailed instruction on the proper way to layer conifer twigs to create a camp bed. And that was a good start. Later came the big blue closed-cell foamy pads, air mattresses and elongated bubble-wrap designs. Now, in only a few years, we're equipped with the ultimate camp mattress — the Therm-a-rest. This invention revolutionized how well we sleep at night.

The story goes that two engineers and enthusiastic hikers from Seattle — John Burroughs and Lim Lea — turned their talents to creating a better sleeping pad because they found themselves laid off and had nothing else better to do. The lack of insulation from and padding against the cold ground were the main shortcomings in what was already commercially available. What inspired their idea of the "Therm-a-rest" was a simple kneeling pad used out in the garden, built of open cell foam and covered with a perforated polyurethane cover. Experimentation with a secondhand sandwich grill, they built the prototype, fusing the two layers together, and that led to a self-inflating pad.

Many campers still start out purchasing the cheaper closed-cell foamy pad or turn blue trying to blow up an air mattress. But eventually all cave in and buy a Therm-a-rest or some knockoff, and finally find an answer to the number one concern that campers have been mumbling about for years while cocooned in their sleeping bags — a good night's sleep.

If Kyla only knew the discomforts campers had to endure before the invention of the Therm-a-rest in 1971.

Some Like It Hot

In attempts to keep campers warm and cozy, there have been a number of gadgets tried that miserably failed. Here are a few memorable ones.

- In 1909, a fuel-burning furnace was worn as a belt and came complete with a water hose and helmet that vented the hot air. Combustion and getting wet simultaneously made the invention a bad idea.

- In 1916, bladder-lined gum-boots were filled with hot liquid.

- In 1969, the Nuclear Corp's "fluid recirculating personal heating system" powered by, not surprisingly, radioactive fuel.

STAYING WARM AND COZY

I just couldn't resist getting in just one more trip before the season ended and the lakes froze. So, on the third weekend of October, when everyone was glued to their television watching reality shows, I invited a neighbor to go on a post-fall canoe trip. I'll admit it was darn cold, and the sun only came out once or twice. In fact, it rained and then snowed most of the time we were out. But we were out, and that in itself was worth numbing our fingers and toes.

The worst weather was the rain, a cold rain that tried relentlessly to soak every piece of gear we had brought along. Once we finally stopped for the day, preparing a dry camp was the ultimate reward.

I have found that the best way to keep everything dry, especially while out paddling and portaging, is to first store items in a number of waterproof bags. I don't mean garbage bags. Even if you're using heavy-duty plastic bags, they will eventually tear open. I'm talking about well-constructed dry bags you buy from high-quality outdoor stores, or, to save you money, heavy-duty plastic placed between two nylon sacks.

I start off by placing my waterproof liner inside my regular pack, with the liner over-sized for the pack to give plenty of length to roll up and secure

Down Versus Synthetic

	Down Sleeping Bags	Synthetic Sleeping Bags
Advantages	• Light weight • Extremely compactible • Very cozy and warm	• Reasonably priced • Contemporary high-tech materials are excellent quality (PrimaLoft, Thermolite, Polarguard) • Streamlined • Not totally useless if it gets wet
Disadvantages	• Expensive • Prone to clumping, which leaves cold spots • If wet, utterly useless • Has an odd odor, especially when wet	• Cheaper models are a waste of money in cold temperatures • Not as compactable as down • Not as cozy as down • Temperature ratings (good to −30 degrees) too good to be true

A totally waterproof bag or barrel is great for keeping gear dry.

at the top. Or better yet, I use a totally waterproof bag, like NRS Bill's Dry Bag. Then, in a number of separate color-coded stuff sacks I place my clothes, sleeping bag, first-aid kit/repair kit, and anything else that's important to keep dry.

My food is either stored in a regular barrel pack or one or two of those smaller olive barrels slipped inside a Duluth-style pack. The large blue barrel is my wife's favorite, as long as she has a top-of-the-line harness for it. The smaller olive barrel stuffed in a regular pack, with a sleeping pad placed between the barrel and your back, is a much cheaper solution, though. You can buy these barrels at some outdoor stores or find your own, free of charge. I visit any place that buys olives in bulk (large-chain grocery stores, delicatessens and restaurants) and either ask for them or wait until garbage day and pick them out of their recycle bin. Make sure to stay away from mushroom barrels. They look similar but will leak if submerged.

My neighbor and I had little trouble keeping warm during the day, as long as we kept moving. But the night air brought a bone-numbing chill. The first thing we did to battle the cold was to set up camp early. Daylight is greatly shortened during the off season and we didn't want to get caught shuffling about in the dark putting the tent up. During setup we munched on high-calorie snacks and made sure to change into dry, warm clothes and keep the heat in by pulling on a wool toque. I take this routine quite seriously

Sweet dreams!

and keep an extra dry pair of long underwear and socks in the front pouch of my parka.

Camping during the off season, I tend to avoid designated summer campsites because they receive so much use that tent sites become far too exposed and firewood is limited. As well, my tent choice for such a trip is always a four-season design that provides plenty of ventilation. Condensation is a major problem in cold temperatures, as it forms quite easily from your breathing and causes the interior of the tent to become uncomfortably damp. Placing the tent on a slight rise will also keep dampness away and using a good thick foam pad to sleep on, not an air mattress, will reduce loss of body heat. I also label an empty water bottle and place it inside the tent to pee in. A full bladder robs the body of more heat than an empty one; and besides, who wants to crawl out in the cold night air to relieve themselves at some ungodly hour.

Fluffing your sleeping bag (a top-of-the line, high-quality four-season design) before crawling in is a good idea. The action creates more air space between the fibers or feathers. If you find yourself shivering inside your sleeping bag, put on your rain gear to act as a vapor barrier and hold in your body heat. Better yet, use a liner to increase the efficiency of your sleeping bag. Or even better, double up two sleeping bags and share your warmth with a partner; which by the way, if you're wondering, I didn't do with my neighbor — not that there's anything wrong with that.

KEEP IT CLEAN

Charlie Brown: "Pig Pen," why are you so dirty? When in the world are you going to clean up?

Pig Pen: I have affixed to me the dirt and dust of countless ages...who am I to disturb history?
— *Peanuts* cartoon, 1954

I'm not sure where the desire comes from, to get dirty and stay dirty while out on a camping trip. Men especially are afflicted by this. Of course, I realize there are times I give off a bad smell myself; sometimes it's intentional so the bugs won't bug me so much. But that doesn't mean I've stopped brushing my teeth or combing my hair. There are a scary number of campers who get totally out of hand with the lack of hygiene. It's as if smelling worse than everyone else is a badge of honor, or a kind of initiation necessary to spending time in the woods.

Alana and Kyla practice good camp hygiene.

A Perfect Toiletry Kit

- Biodegradable soap
- Biodegradable shampoo
- Hand sanitizer
- Baby wipes
- Baby powder
- Lip balm
- Tweezers

- Toothbrush
- Toothpaste or baking soda
- Toilet paper (1 roll per five days)
- Sunscreen lotion
- Birth control
- Hand moisturizer

Laundry day becomes necessary by day ten.

Packing a pair of socks per day is not overdoing it.

Two major problems can occur with slacking off on being clean, however (three if you include banishment from the rest of the group). Not keeping fresh is, assuming you aren't like this at home, a sign that you're just waiting to get back to civilization to get sanitary again, which means you're fighting the process of becoming comfortable out on a trip. This can cause problems with group dynamics and self esteem. The cleaner you keep yourself the more comfortable you feel and the longer you can go without becoming homesick. More important, however, you open yourself up to becoming seriously ill. At home we keep ourselves dirt free, so the moment your hygiene routine falters, germs can move in and have a heyday.

On the other hand, there are campers who scrupulously continue their grooming routines, even to the extent of bringing along cosmetics and body sprays. There's really no need for it, and bears have been know to be attracted to some perfumes, but I generally don't harass anyone who packs things like deodorant or even eyeliner. As long as they carry the extra weight, if keeping their delightful appearance also allows them to fight off parasites related to Montezuma, all the better for them.

One pair of socks a day is also not excessive. Your feet are what get you around out there and you definitely don't want mess with that. And a pair of underwear for every second day isn't a bad idea either or a good supply of alcohol wipes to keep you fresh and clean down there.

Hand sanitizing with alcohol liquid gel is something you should be religious about. Washing up at the shoreline and then wiping wet hands on your pant legs is not a good way to defend yourself (and your traveling partners) from nasty parasites.

Portable Shower

A shower seems to be the one comfort campers miss the most. Why not pack along a portable shower? A few designs are on the market and one can easily be made with a water jug and plastic hose. The portable showers sold at outdoor stores consist of a plastic bag or collapsible container strong enough to hold water. A hose is attached at the base, making up the shower head. Since it is solar energy that heats up the water inside, the bag should have one side made of clear plastic and the other black. It's a simply process. Hang the bag in a tree, allowing the sunlight to penetrate the clear plastic side and allowing the black side to absorb and radiate the heat.

Sleeping bags should be aired out every two or three days, dirty clothes should be stored in a separate stuff sack and laundry day should be declared every five or six days.

Spreading out our towels to dry each morning is my wife's major weapon against mildew taking over and indirectly adding to your body odor. Her obsession not only kept us smelling fresh on a twelve-day canoe trip down northern Ontario's Steel River, it also gave us the privilege of labeling a particular rapid en route. On the morning of day eight, Alana placed our towel out over the packs as usual and shortly after lost it overboard while we blindly went through a Class Three rapid not marked on our map. I wrote the lost towel story up in a publication and noticed two years later a government map had been released with our "Lost Towel Rapid" marked on it. Sounds trivial but I think that's really cool.

POOPING PERFECTLY IN THE WOODS

When guys in camouflage pants and hunting hats sat around in the Four Aces Diner talking about fearsome things done out-of-doors, I would no longer have to feel like such a cupcake. I wanted a little of that swagger that comes with being able to gaze at a far horizon through eyes of chipped granite and say with a slow, manly sniff, "Yeah, I've shit in the woods."
— Bill Bryson, *A Walk in the Woods*

No one seems to want to want to talk about this but a poop properly disposed of behind camp can make or break the group dynamics during any trip. To start, before the spot is chosen and the trousers are dropped, a proper camp attitude must be set or you'll have turd anarchy. Laugh about it, share stories about it, and more important, make it common knowledge that excreting waste from your bowels is a natural occurrence that all

No one seems to want to talk about this, but waste of the human kind properly (or improperly) disposed of behind camp can make or break the group dynamics during any trip.

Dirty Business

- Write up a poop plan and stick to it.
- Regulate a safe distance traveled in the backwoods before any feces is actually released into the wilds (it should be at least 50 meters).
- Place a bag containing communal TP, hand sanitizer, small spade, and favorite paddling magazine hanging on a tree limb (a bag missing from the limb symbolizes that the forest is presently occupied).
- If there's an already developed treasure chest (thunder box, candy box, outhouse...etc.) available, then it should be agreed upon that everyone makes use if it.
- If no outhouse is available, then the spade is used to dig a "cat-hole" (the process of turning up the first inch or two (3–4 cm) of topsoil and, when finished, covering up the excrement with a mound of dirt, just as a cat does in the litter box (cat-holes are much more efficient in breaking the manure down to potting soil than the Boy Scout routine of a deeply dug trench).
- Announce to everyone back at camp that it was a success and add detailed information on the position used (a simple squat, over a log, back up against a tree...etc.)
- Return, very carefully, with the wad of TP and discreetly, or not discreetly, dispose of it in a very hot campfire.
- Wait at least ten minutes before toasting marshmallows.

Treasure Chest, Thunder Box, Poop Collector ... whatever you call it, if there's one at the campsite it's always a good idea to make use of it.

members of the group can and may do at any given time of the day, but that the disposal of it must be done in an environmentally responsible matter. Sounds silly, but the more you keep the act of pooping a private session, the more accidental displacement of poop you'll have at camp.

Some people are a little shy when it comes to performing, however. The record of holding in poop must go to a canoe mate of mine who, for some bizarre reason, refuses to do number two while camping out. He once held it in for five full days while we paddled Quebec's Dumoine River. Of course, the moment he got to my house my fellow paddler ran upstairs, dropped his trousers and let loose what he had been holding on to for an entire week. No surprise, the toilet overflowed and the calamity was immediately noticed by my wife who was setting the table for dinner downstairs when she saw a mixture of water and, well, poop seeping through the chandelier.

Alana didn't hold back her feelings and yelled at my buddy to next time go poop in the forest before coming to our house. For me, it was just a good reason to have him help drywall the ceilings and an excuse to tease him endlessly to the day I die. Every Christmas since the terrible incident I have mailed him a gift consisting of a mini plunger and Kathleen Myer's excellent book *How to Shit in the Woods*.

SAUNA SWEAT IS THE BEST SWEAT

It all started innocently enough. I was guiding a group of Europeans on a canoe trip in Temagami, Ontario, and we found ourselves windbound for the entire day, and growing bored by the minute. We tried a number of card games and told stories and jokes twice and even three times over. Things were getting desperate, though, so I sprang into action by suggesting we build a sauna along a nearby beach to help pass the time away.

Everyone seemed enthusiastic at getting a chance to sweat out their aching muscles and release their frustrations of being stuck at camp. So I initiated the design layout and construction, even though it was my first attempt at building a sauna and I was merely working from memory of an article I had read on the subject over a year ago.

The collection of wood for the frame was the first on our checklist. Saplings would have been nice to use but the site we were camped on had seen enough abuse from past residents so we made the decision to use deadfall for the frame instead.

A hoop design or cabin-type structure would be ideal but because all of us lacked the expertise we went with a simple teepee design. Three wood poles were lashed together with rope and then a tent fly was draped over the structure, with the corner points of the nylon cover being staked or held down with small boulders. The door was just an opening in the corner of the tarp.

Construction was done on a beach, which made the second step far easier. A small pit was dug in the center of the makeshift sauna, approximately a foot deep and a foot wide. A second firepit was also built outside of the sauna where medium-size rocks were buried in hot coals. Once the rocks were red hot, they were carefully brought into the sauna pit where a pot of water was ready to be poured over them.

Next was the fun part. The group was gathered and readied to step inside in an orderly fashion. And since I was the one who initiated it all, I was given the honor to enter first.

That's when things got interesting. My naïve assumption was that campers making use of saunas should be naked. Heck, I didn't even second guess my decision to go nude because the group I was guiding was all European. So I crawled in, removed my towel and sat there cross-legged waiting for everyone to enter. And they did, all clothed!

How embarrassing. It was a scene I never want to relive. The worst part wasn't really being caught naked. It was having to stay in the sauna, chatting away about nothing in particular but staying put long enough so that when I did make an exit it didn't appear to be out of awkwardness.

Would I do it again? Definitely, in a heartbeat. A homemade sauna is one of the most rewarding activities you can do on a camping trip. The only thing I'd change would be to be the last person in, so I'd have a chance to check out what everyone is wearing before I decided to drop the towel.

Heating up the sauna rocks at Temagami, Ontario.

Sauna Etiquette

The sauna is an ancient custom in Finland. It was perceived to be a very holy place where women would give birth, the sick would go to be healed and the dead would be washed before burial. Each sauna was also believed to house a gnome or sauna elf who would punish people who behaved improperly — the sauna is not the place to argue, make loud noises, sleep, or be "immoral."

- Keep the noise down; to most people a sauna is a place of peace and quiet to contemplate the meaning of life.

- Even though it was fun in the gym locker room back in high school, no snapping of towels on someone's bare skin.

- No laughing at any man's "shrinkage" after, or even before, the celebratory dip in the cold lake.

- Know the difference between being nude and naked; if everyone saunters around with nothing on then you're all "nude" but if one person has a bathing suit on or towel wrapped around them, then everyone else feels vulnerable and "naked."

- No gawking, gazing, staring or even peeking at other's private parts — unless you have full consent to do so by the person.

- Don't pull an Elaine from the sitcom *Seinfeld* and "accidentally" bump into someone to find out of they have a fake boob-job. It's a waste of time anyway since most campers don't get boob-jobs.

SKINNY DIPPING

I should never have done it if Eddie had not insisted
that according to the standard text-books the day in every
well-ordered camp always began with this ceremony.
Not to take the morning dip, he said, was to manifest a
sad lack of the true camping spirit.
— Albert Bigelow Paine, *The Tent Dwellers* (1908)

For the record, I'm not what one would call a nudist. I don't sleep in the nude or hang around camp exposing myself to the elements. I just choose to swim without any clothes on. I always have. There's a sense of freedom one gets plunging into a cold lake in early morning without the restriction of swim trunks. In fact, I'd go as far as to say that the act of skinny dipping is as much a part of a camping trip as toasting marshmallow or watching the sun set. And it was the act of bathing nude that actually started my writing career.

I was on a solo canoe trip in northern Ontario, Killarney Park, to be exact, and after a long day of paddling and portaging I thought a swim was in order. So, it was off with the clothes and a quick leap into the water. While in the downward arc of a deep dive I felt the water tremble, definitely an odd

"Full moon" over Quetico Lake.

feeling that made me quickly come back up to the surface. And there, skimming the surface, was a water bomber collecting a load of water to douse a nearby forest fire.

I panicked a little, of course. There I was, alone in the wilderness with trees burning nearby. So I immediately exited the lake and climbed the highest rock point behind camp to scout for any signs of danger.

This was a moment I'll never forget. There I was, standing on an exposed ridge wearing nothing but my birthday suit, one hand holding onto a stout white pine and the other cupped above my eyes to knock out the sun's glare as I searched the horizon for smoke or flames. A second later I heard a giggle from below and one of six girls from a canoe camp that was paddling by yelled out "Hey, there's a naked man up there!"

My response was immediate and silly. I quickly ran down the ridge toward camp. On the way, however, I took a tumble, splitting my knee wide open.

The camp leader saw me topple down the rock and gave a command to paddle into my camp to administer first aid. She was a gorgeous blonde clad in a tan bikini and if I wasn't naked I would have definitely wanted treatment from her. But again I panicked, told the girls I was okay and that there was no need to approach. The attractive camp counselor called the girls off and as they paddled across the lake I could hear their laughing and giggling echo across the water.

I managed to dress the wound, and dress myself as well, and then wrote up the incident in my journal that evening. I mailed the same script that I put in my journal to my local newspaper when I got back home in hopes of being published. They ran the story the next day, titling it "Northern Exposure." In return I received a payment of $60 and the beginning of my career writing silly stories that incriminate me as an expert skinny-dipping outdoorsman.

Skinny-Dipping Etiquette

- When group dipping, make sure everyone is in agreement to see and be seen.
- Think twice before agreeing to skinny dip with a prospective mother-in-law or boss or with your friend's spouse.
- Undress where ever you please but please warn everyone around you that you're about to undress.
- Skinny dipping by moonlight is an age-old tradition but keep in mind that during a full moon things can be seen a lot more clearly than you might like.
- Swim well out of range of other campsites.
- Know that there is a big difference between swimming naked with a group and standing around nude chatting with everyone after the dip.
- Be extra mindful of personal space issues; bumping into another's nakedness isn't always considered a good thing.
- Keep in mind that being nude with someone else should not be considered an invitation for sex; that's a totally different camping element.
- Cameras should always be off limits unless permission to take pictures is given.
- Skinny dipping is not a good time to joke about anyone's fear of murky water, leeches, jelly fish or their own physical insecurities.
- Never make your less-than-perfect figure be the reason for not giving skinny dipping a try.
- Whatever the downfalls, you should try skinny dipping at least once in your life!

6

EATING WELL

"When you wake up in the morning, Pooh," said Piglet at last, "what's the first thing you say to yourself?"

"What's for breakfast?" said Pooh. "What do you say, Piglet?"

"I say, I wonder what's going to happen exciting today?" said Piglet.

Pooh nodded thoughtfully.

"It's the same thing," he said.

— A.A. Milne, *The House at Pooh Corner*

WHEN IT COMES TO FOOD ON CAMPING TRIPS I'VE SEEN two main types of participants. There are the survivalists who just eat to fuel up, caring little about taste. They stuff down boiled noodles and fill in the gaps with energy bars. Good luck to them if they happen to be out for more than a few days. They're sure to crash. Then there are the campers who live to eat. They take great pleasure in outdoing someone else's recipe and would far rather plan and prepare their own meals than purchase prepackaged camp food. To them, a long trip is a welcome challenge, not something to endure until you get back to the world of fast food restaurants.

I'm not a noodles and energy bar person. I dry my own food, take loving care in putting proper measured amounts into separate zip-lock bags, labeled and sorted for its particular day of the trip. And I go into great detail when typing out the ingredients and recipe instructions on a tiny piece of paper placed inside each bag. Some may call it a food fixation, but my camping partners call it dedication to having a good trip.

My guiding days taught me the importance of having good food along on a trip. Not just nutritious food. That's a given if you want to keep energy levels up. But the fancier the recipes the more positive the group seemed to

Yum! Blueberry pancakes for breakfast. Alana Callan, Temagami.

What the Voyageurs Ate

"Leading a laborious and hazardous life, in a country destitute of game, they generally subsist upon maize boiled with fat. The maize is first cleared of its husk and then boiled in water. One quart of prepared grain, and two ounces of melted suet, from the usual ration of an Engagé, unless pemmican can be procured. We were likewise obliged to live for a long while upon this unpalatable food; the only variety we had was a sort of hasty pudding; made with meal and buffalo grease, and seasoned with service berry."

— William H. Keating, *Narrative of an Expedition to the Source of St. Peter's River (1730)*

be; the more glamorous the better. I'd start off with hors d'oeuvres made of pita bread fried in olive oil and garlic, topped with a white cheese, and dipped in salsa and tabouli mix, served with a cocktail. The main meal would consist of regular fare, usually pasta or rice dish, but with fancy sauces and an even fancier names given to it. And dessert was extra special. Forget brownies. One of my specialties was a double-layered fudge cake with a raspberry center topped with white frosting and shaved chocolate. If you served up a meal like that, especially halfway through the trip, you'd definitely have repeat customers.

So, do yourself a favor and renounce the days of a hot cereal mush for breakfast, stale crackers and moldy cheese for lunch and macaroni and cheese for dinner. Make each meal a fancy affair and I guarantee your trips will change for the better.

RECIPE CONTEST

If you want to spice up your trip and the food you bring along, I strongly suggest a friendly camp cook-off competition for the first night out and the last night out.

Start by placing everyone in small cooking groups (of two people is best but it may work with three or four if the size of the main group itself is larger). Then choose a judge who agrees to sample everyone's meal and also agrees not to accept any bribes (trust me, this is vital).

Prizes then must be rewarded to the winning group and a major punishment handed out to the losing group, both for the first night and the last night. And you guessed it; the last night's meal is definitely more challenging. Food isn't fresh and recipes are more of the trial and error type.

In my regular group of campers our first meal motivation is that the worst dinner created has the cooks doing dishes for the remainder of the trip. And the loser for the last meal has to hand over their remaining spirits (rum, scotch, vodka...) to the rest of the group. Sounds serious? It is. But boy, have we made some darn good meals because of it.

"Snack time!" Alana and Kyla harvest a few wild blueberries at Chiniguchi Lake.

Here are the winning recipes for the first meal contest from the past couple of years.

Parsnip and Pancetta Pasta

1–2 medium sized parsnips (peeled, quartered, cored and cut
   crosswise into small pieces)
6 slices of pancetta
2 cups water
a pinch of salt
2 tablespoons butter or olive oil
a handful of egg fettuccini noodles
1 tablespoon dried (or fresh) parsley
$\frac{1}{2}$ cup parmesan

1. Fry up pancetta until brown and take out of pan.
2. On medium heat, add butter or oil to frying pan and cook up parsnips until lightly browned (approximately 12 minutes). Remove from heat.
3. Boil pasta in a pot of salted water and then drain pasta but keep 1 cup of pasta water.
4. Add pasta and $\frac{1}{2}$ cup pasta water to parsnips. Mix in chopped-up pancetta and parsley and place on moderate heat for 1 minute. Add more pasta water if necessary.
5. Garnish with parmesan cheese.

A good camp cook should be treated like royalty on a trip.

The more you eat, the less you have to carry.

Thai Coconut Chicken

2 cups jasmine rice
3 cups water
1 tablespoon olive oil
2 pieces frozen boneless chicken breasts
1 tablespoon curry powder
6 asparagus sprouts
1 cup snow peas
$\frac{1}{2}$ cup shredded carrots
1 red onion
1 can coconut milk
* *everything except the can of coconut milk can be dehydrated for a meal later in the trip*

1. Boil rice in water and let simmer for 20 minutes.
2. Place chicken and curry powder in a zip-lock bag and shake to coat chicken.
3. Cook chicken in oiled pan over medium heat for 4–5 minutes. Then mix in the chopped-up asparagus and onion, shredded carrots, and snow peas; cook for another 3 minutes.
4. Pour in coconut milk and continue cooking until sauce has heated up and chicken is cooked through.
5. Serve all on a bed of rice.

Sometimes leftovers can be a blessing in surprise. Andy Baxter makes a "surprise" breakfast dish.

Lobster Pasta

1 large can of lobster (or 1 whole frozen lobster)
4 tablespoons butter
1 medium white onion
3 garlic gloves
1 28 oz. can of diced tomatoes (or substitute with dehydrated tomatoes)
4 tablespoons olive oil
2 large pinches of salt
a pinch of pepper
1 tablespoon ground cinnamon
1 cup white sauce (3 tablespoons white flour, 1 tablespoons powdered milk
   and 1 cup water)
2 handfuls of dried spaghetti
1 tablespoon dried parsley

1. Boil frozen lobster in pot of water for 6-8 minutes. Or if you have just a
   can of lobster then add that to a large frying pan in the 3 tablespoons of
   butter and place on medium heat, adding 2 garlic gloves and chopped
   onion.
2. Boil another pot of water, with added salt, for the spaghetti. Cook until
   tender (approximately 8 minutes) and drain.
3. Add tomatoes to the frying pan and increase heat for the juice to boil.
   Then add the olive oil, salt, pepper and cinnamon.
4. Cook for 5–7 minutes, stirring constantly, and then slowly stir in white
   sauce for another 2–3 minutes on low heat.
5. Stir in leftover butter and garlic to spaghetti and pour on lobster and
   sauce; garnish with parsley.

Always remember to remove your bug net before dinner.

Ashley's Chili-Lime Roasted Corn on the Cob

Corn on the cob makes an amazing camp meal. The only drawback is the bulk of the corn cobs in your pack. This is why we have it the first night out. And this is one awesome way my buddy Ashley McBride makes it.

juice of one lime
2 tablespoons olive oil
1 teaspoon chili powder
a pinch of salt and pepper
2 cobs of corn (per person)
a square of tin foil big enough to roll up each cob

1. Let the campfire burn down to hot coals.
2. Squeeze the lime juice into a large zip-lock bag and add the olive oil, chili powder, salt and pepper. Seal the bag and shake.
3. Place the cob of corn on the sheet of tin foil, turn up the ends and corners, and then squeeze the contents of the zip-lock bag onto the corn cob (save a little of the juicy stuff to pour on after the cob is baked in the fire).
4. Poke a hole in the aluminum foil wrapper and roast the corn cob in the bed of coals for 8–10 minutes.

Buried Treasure Bananas

This may seem too simple a camp recipe to win any prizes but when you have my three-year-old daughter the judge, and her mom the cook, it's bound to be a winner.

1 large banana for each person, slightly underripe
a handful of mini marshmallows or a couple of large ones cut into pieces
1 cup milk chocolate pieces
1/2 teaspoon cinnamon

1. Place a banana on a flat surface and pull back a strip of the peel
2. Cut a V wedge trench the full length of the banana and discard (or eat) the removed section.
3. Fill in the trench with marshmallow and chocolate pieces, sprinkle with cinnamon and place the strip of peel back
4. Roll the banana in tin foil, seal the edges and bake in the coals of the campfire for 8–10 minutes.
5. Remove from heat and let cool before eating.

Following are the winning recipes for the last meal contest from the past couple of years.

Cedar-Smoked Beet Salad

This was my recipe. Well, I got the basic idea from some magazine stored beside the toilet at home. But it tasted good and looked darn impressive when I prepared it.

6 medium-sized beets
a handful of fresh white cedar boughs
a few strips of birchbark
2 cups water
1 tablespoon cider vinegar
$\frac{1}{4}$ cup balsamic vinegar
1 garlic clove
2 teaspoons dried parsley
$\frac{1}{4}$ cup olive oil
$1\frac{1}{2}$ teaspoons dried mustard
pinch of salt and pepper
1 small red cabbage
$\frac{1}{2}$ cup cashew or toasted hazelnuts
$\frac{1}{2}$ cup raisins
1 carrot

1. Place beets in 2 cups salted water and bring to a boil. Reduce heat and simmer for 15–20 minutes or until beets are firm but can easily be poked with a fork.
2. Place the beets in a tin foil square with the edges folded up and a few holes poked in the bottom. (A grill basket works better than the tin foil if you don't have to carry it far.) Cut off the end branches of the cedar bough and cover the beets and place the birch bark evenly throughout the beets. Ignite the birch bark and allow to cedar to flame and smoke until it's completely burned.
3. Blow off the ash and thinly slice the beets.
4. For dressing, mix up the cider and balsamic vinegar, shredded garlic, olive oil, mustard, parsley, salt and pepper.
5. Shred red cabbage and carrot, place beets on top, pour salad dressing and garnish with nuts and raisins.

Sweet and Sour Beef Jerky Stir Fry

Anne Ostrom made this recipe up for us on the last night of the Kopka River, in northwestern Ontario. It was my first time tripping with Anne and I must admit I was a little worried about her cooking abilities. During the three weeks our group was out it seemed she had snacked on nothing but tofu and dried peas. Anne is very health conscious and she took some teasing from us guys. But when she cooked up this meal for everyone on the last evening, the kidding ceased immediately and now I'm begging her to be lead cook on our next trip together.

2 cups white rice
20–24 slices of homemade teriyaki beef jerky (use inside round steak
    if possible)
6 dehydrated pineapple rings cut into chunks (do not use the candied
    pineapple available in bulk food stores)
2–3 dehydrated peppers, sliced (or approximately ¾ cup dehydrated
    pepper flakes from a bulk food store)
½ cup dried mushrooms (chinese, shiitake, or oyster)
4 tablespoons dehydrated onion flakes (from a bulk food store)

¼ cup soy sauce
¼ cup brown sugar
3 tablespoons cornstarch
½ teaspoon dried ginger
½ teaspoon garlic powder
3 tablespoons oil

1. Rehydrate dried ingredients (from jerky to onion flakes in the ingredient list) for about 1 hour in hot water: As soon as you get into camp put jerky, etc. into a large frying pan or pot and add 3–4 cups water to just cover the food. Bring to boil, turn off heat, and let soak while you set up camp. You are ready to start cooking when the jerky is tender.
2. Fry the rehydrated food: Drain the meat, etc., saving the liquid in a pot or 1L bottle. Add oil and fry until the meat and veggies are almost cooked, about 10 minutes.
3. Mix the sauce while the meat is frying: First, taste the saved liquid (3–4 cups). It will already be sweet and salty. Add 1 tablespoon soy sauce, stir in ¼ cup brown sugar, garlic and ginger powder. Taste again, and add more soy sauce, sugar, or spices as needed.
4. Add ¾ of the sauce to the meat. Add 2–3 tablespoons cornstarch to remaining liquid and mix completely. Add to the meat and heat until sauce is thickened.
5. Serve over rice. (Serves 4)

Vegetarian option: Use TVP instead of jerky, and bring extra soy sauce.

Home-Dried Camp Food

Packing dehydrated meals along on your trips is definitely the way to go if you're trying to keep the weight down. But creating homemade recipes rather than buying those pre-packed meals is the preferred choice when considering cost and flavor. You may think dehydrated food doesn't make for great meals, but try a few recipes and you'll see how you can enjoy five-star dining under the stars with all the ingredients weighing much less than they do when you carry them home from the grocery store. For multi-trips or one major expedition, buying a food dehydrator is definitely the best bet. The expense isn't justified, however, if you're just doing just one or two trips a season. That's when your conventional oven makes more sense. Here are a few tips:

- Solids such as fruit, veggies and turkey-jerky are placed directly on the oven racks and sauces go on a on a cookie sheet, coated with spray-on Pam or a layer of wax paper.
- The dehydration process removes water, not fat or grease. To keep meat from going rancid, pre-cook it and rinse well with a spaghetti drainer and hot tap water.
- Place items in oven at the lowest temperature it will go (usually 150° F).
- Prop the oven door open with a toothpick to encourage some air to circulate and moisture to escape, and then wait 6–10 hours, depending on the water content of whatever you're drying.
- At camp, simply place the contents into ¼ cup of boiling water and watch it transform to its original form.

From left to right, dried tomatoes, salsa sauce, mushrooms, and red and yellow peppers.

Roast Lake Trout

I can't tell you who made up this recipe but I can tell you it's darn good. I came upon some paddlers from Minnesota while traveling through Ontario's Quetico Park and they invited me in for a snack of roast laker. I was intrigued, so I drifted to shore and sampled their dinner. Wow! I've never had lake trout taste so good. Of course, they never did give me their names, or the recipe, for that matter — but I think this is how they made it.

1 medium-size lake trout — gutted, not filleted
1 small walleye fillet (or walleye cheeks if you have them)
2 fresh lemons
1 medium white onion
a few good pinches lemon pepper spice
1 McIntosh apple sliced into chunks
1 cup butter (it seems like a lot, but you want it to be deep-fried)

1. Gut and behead the lake trout and lay it on top a square of tin foil.
2. Fill the cavity of the lake trout with the cut up lemon, apples, onion, butter, and walleye. (The apples help keep the meat moist while baking.)
3. Sprinkle on lemon pepper, wrap fish up in tin foil and place in hot coals for 20–30 minutes, turning it over halfway through.
4. Remove from fire, open tin foil and peel or flake off meat (skin will stick to foil).

Campfire Cooking Tips

- Small fires are easier and better to cook on.
- Avoid direct flame since it will burn the outside of food but keep the inside uncooked.
- Wait until the wood has burned down to embers.
- Increase the cooking heat by piling the coals closer together and reduce it by spreading them apart.
- A blanket of ash covering the coals acts as an insulator and controls the heat better for cooking, especially potatoes, corn or onions wrapped in tin foil.
- To reduce smoke, try burning dried wood from a beaver lodge; it's sun-dried with no resin or outer bark, reducing smoke in a big way.
- Softwoods such as pine and spruce may be good to get the fire started but hardwoods such as maple or oak are a far better heat for cooking.
- A camp grill works better than trying to balance pots on a stick hanging over the fire.
- Build a windbreak with rocks.
- Use the edge of the fire to keep items already cooked warm while you prepare the rest of the meal.

Fish Fajitas

My canoe buddy Andy Baxter couldn't fish if his life depended on it. Mind you, that doesn't mean he doesn't catch fish. This guy has the worst fishing rod money can buy, a broken reel, good-for-nothing lures and an inability to properly land a fish once he's hooked it. But he somehow manages to still win the first fish and the biggest fish awards each year (winner gets a bottle of booze from the loser — me). He also wins the best fish recipe. Here it is:

4 walleye, bass or pike fillets
6 tortillas
1 medium to large white onion
pinch of chili powder
pinch of paprika
1 cup butter, margarine or cooking oil (it seems like a lot, but you want it to
   be deep-fried)
$\frac{1}{2}$ cup shredded white cheese
1 cup dehydrated salsa sauce
1 clove garlic

1. Reconstitute salsa sauce in $\frac{1}{2}$ cup boiling water.
2. Place frying pan over moderate heat and add butter, margarine or cooking oil.
3. Add chopped white onion and fish fillets to pan.
4. Add chili powder, paprika and reconstituted salsa sauce on top of fish and flip to cook other side; fish is done when flesh begins falling or flaking apart.
5. Serve in a tortilla with cheese sprinkled on top and possibly extra salsa sauce added.

Getting to enjoy fresh fish on a trip is well worth the hassle of packing along rod, reel and tackle.

Len Lockwood prepares his famous double-layer chocolate cake on day of five of the Dumoine River, Quebec.

BAKING IN THE BUSH

In the 1943 book *The Incomplete Anglers,* the author, John D. Robins, sharply criticizes his paddling partner during a trip across Ontario's Algonquin Park for toasting the bread before its time. Traditionally it was forbidden to toast bread until a week or so into a trip, simply because by then it was going stale and moldy. Toasting it was a good way to get a few more days out of it.

The question is, why didn't they bake their own while on the trip? There's really no excuse not to bake fresh bread, or anything else for that matter, while camping out. Reflector ovens were definitely around at the time of Robins' trip and are still used today; Dutch ovens have become common in many outdoor kitchen sets; and a product called the Outback Oven has revolutionized the process of baking up brownies, cakes and pies.

Many campers are simply afraid of baking, especially bread. Baking is a little more complicated affair than pan-frying bannock. And it takes up a lot of time and fuel. But the golden brown top of a loaf is a heavenly sight, and the sweet aroma of the first slice is pure bliss.

Practice does make the perfect loaf, of course. And to be an expert, extra care has to be given during the crucial step of mixing in the leavening agent to the dough, which is what "puffs it up." The kneading process (mixing the leavening agent and then punching the heck out of the dough with your fist) is necessary to create tiny bubbles and allow the dough to rise.

Baking powder or baking soda work as well but only under heat and they react only during the baking process. For pre-baking agents, however, yeast is the most common. When yeast is added, a chemical reaction occurs that releases gas slowly throughout the mixture of dough, which in turn gets trapped and in an attempt to escape forces the dough to rise. Yeast needs warmth to produce the gas and the best source while camping is sunlight (warm coals of a campfire could be used in a pinch). The yeast is also activated by lukewarm water and sugar.

Small packets of yeast are perfect to take along camping. Simply sprinkle the desired amount (one small packet per loaf of bread) over 1 cup of lukewarm water (the temperature of bath water), add a couple of pinches of sugar, mix and then set aside in a warm place until you're ready to mix the dough (flour and water). When the yeast is frothy and expanding, it is good to use.

Sourdough is an even more traditional leavening agent. The bread gets its name from the flour and water mixture having already begun to ferment. The fermenting process creates a breeding ground for microscopic organisms which in turn produce carbon dioxide gas. This foul concoction, with its characteristic "sour" smell, is called the "starter." Sourdough bread was popular during the Klondike when yeast was impossible to keep fresh. It could be replenished each and every time it was used. In fact, a Klondiker's "starter" could literally be passed down from generation to generation (it

Lemon cake baked on an Outback Oven.

now possible to purchase dried starter at a bulk food and health food store) or you could begin your own smelly brew.

To prepare the sourdough bread starter before to your trip, heat up a cup of milk and add a cup of water. Let it cool to lukewarm. Then mix a tablespoon of sugar, teaspoon of salt and two cups of flour. Make sure to use a large bowl for mixing because the ingredients are going to expand. Place a towel over the bowl and store it in a warm place for 4–5 days (or until it has that frothy appearance). Then let it sit in room temperature for another 5 days, stirring it up daily and ignoring how it looks and smells — the more foul the odor the better the bread will be, actually.

Keep it in a jar in the fridge until the day before you leave on your trip.

Baking in the Bush

You don't need any of the fancier gadgets to bake, as long as you packed two pots and a plastic bag. Here's how to do it.

- In a heavy-duty freezer zip-lock bag mix flour, sugar, yeast, dry powdered milk, oil and hot water.

- Squeeze upper part of bag to force out the air and then shake and work bag with fingers to blend ingredients.

- Remove from bag and knead on floured surface.

- Place formed bread back in bag and let it rise for ten minutes.

- Fill the larger of the two pots with 1 inch of water, then rest second pot on top of water (this acts as a heat diffuser).

- Place the bagged bread in the smaller pot and loosely roll down the top of the bag (don't seal it).

- Place a lid on the larger pot and boil until the bread is baked (should take 20–30 minutes).

Carrot cake baking in a traditional reflector oven.

Bannock is one of the simplest things to prepare on a camping trip.

Basic Bannock

Bannock is even more traditional than sourdough. It's customary for camping trips, though, because it's easier to make. If you can mix and fry up a pancake, you can prepare a batch of bannock. Bannock isn't the best flavored bread, but the trick, of course, is not to tell anyone how simple it is to make and then to smother it with raspberry jam.

½ cup white flour
½ cup whole wheat flour
1 teaspoon baking powder
3 tablespoon powdered milk
½ teaspoon salt

Mix all dry ingredients and add water *slowly* until dough is slightly sticky. Separate into 3–4 patties and fry in an oiled frying pan over moderate heat until both sides are a golden brown.

There's no doubt that the name s'more is short for "some more."

MORE S'MORES

S'mores have been a camp tradition ever since the recipe first appeared in the 1927 edition of the Girl Scout handbook *Tramping and Trailing*. And there's no doubt why it was given its name — short for "some more." Think about it. Kids get to pierce a sugary marshmallow with a stick, hold it over the campfire until it ignites, then squish it between two chunks of chocolate and two graham crackers (some campers have been known to toss the crackers).

Like most classic recipes, the s'more wasn't completely original: similar Moon Pies were introduced in 1917 and Mallomars were on the store shelves as early as 1913. Marshmallows, the key ingredient to a s'more, have an even longer history. Egyptians would squeeze the sweet sap from the mallow plant growing in wild marshes and add honey for flavor. By the mid-1800s the treat had reached France when owners of a small candy store whipped, sweetened and molded the gummy sap.

It didn't take long for the natural mallow to be replaced by gelatin and modified cornstarch. In 1948, a marshmallow manufacturer, Alex Doumark, had the idea of pushing the sticky substance through a long pipe and cutting it to the shape we're used to seeing. A couple of years later some other manufacturer had the idea of injecting air, giving the marshmallow its fluffy, light texture.

To date no one seems to know who actually started the act of toasting a marshmallow over a campfire and transforming the white spongy puff into a burned carbon shell with a sticky, tongue-burning centre. Probably some camp counselor who couldn't stand baking up another can of pork and beans. But it's in the United Stated where most are now consumed, 90 million pounds per year to be exact. The majority of those consumers are — no surprise — under the age of twelve. It seems the older one gets, the less inviting a toasted marshmallow becomes. Most adults, 56 percent in fact, prefer eating it raw. Truth is, many parents secretly loathe the making of s'mores on camping trips. The problem is that the gooey mess will undoubtedly get all over the kids' clothes, making them bear bait for the rest of the evening. So try these not-so-sticky recipes.

S'more Crepes

S'mores are pretty much downgraded versions of a fancy French crepe. Spread Nutella on a soft tortilla, sprinkle icing sugar and coconut shavings, roll up in a piece of tin foil and roast in the campfire or Dutch oven.

Mexican S'more

Spread a generous amount of peanut butter on a soft tortilla shell, add a layer of chocolate chips and mini-marshmallows, then roll up the tortilla. Wrap in tin foil and cook it over a fire grill for just under five minutes. Unwrap and eat with a spoon.

Hershey-Squirt S'mores

Toast the marshmallow over the fire and then, without removing it from the stick, roll in pie plate a quarter full of Hershey's chocolate syrup and crushed graham crackers.

S'more Facts

- August 10 is National S'more Day and is celebrated in the United States.
- The world record for the largest s'more ever made was set on May 23, 2003; it weighed weighing 1,600 pounds and used 20,000 toasted marshmallows and 7,000 chocolate bars.
- The marshmallow capital of the world is in Ligonier, Noble County, Indiana.
- In 2004, capitalizing on all the nostalgia, Hershey's spent $30 million in advertising to introduce the S'mores candy bar.
- Most common alternative ingredients for the outside of a s'more: chocolate-chip cookies, gingersnap cookies, halved Rice Krispies squares, mini croissants, brownies, rice cakes and apple slices.
- Most common alternative ingredients for the inside portion of a s'more: colored mini-marshmallows, peanut butter, Nutella spread, After Eight mints, candied ginger, jelly beans, crushed Reese's Pieces and gummy worms.

BUSH MARTINIS AND OTHER WILDERNESS SPIRITS

A martini is the elixir of quietude.
— E.B. White, author of *Charlotte's Web*

PERSONALLY I THINK A CAMPING TRIP ISN'T THE SAME WITH-out some kind of alcohol. It's not that I'm a big boozer. Truth is, one or two drinks are usually my limit. I learned long ago that waking up with a hangover in a hot, stuffy tent is definitely something to avoid. And most of the time the natural high I get provides a much better stimulant than a couple of drinks. But it seems to me that a glass of wine, a martini, shot of Scotch, or even a splash of Irish cream in the coffee always seems to initiate relaxation time and signal social hour around camp.

There's something to be said for having everyone gather at the end of a long day and pouring spirits in everyone's camp mug. It can really connect a group. And yes, I've traveled with groups that don't bother bringing alcohol and similar feelings can still be achieved with mugs of hot chocolate.

Whatever your tipple, though, it's a given that the further your supplies are reduced, the more priceless the supplies become — and that's when the trip really becomes interesting. I've used rum, whisky or extra cocoa as bar-gaining chips and the only other item in my pack that has had more power is an extra roll of toilet paper. There's also the betting that goes on around camp when alcohol is packed. The biggest fish caught, the most correct

The fancier the drink, the better the reaction from your fellow campers.

correct weather prediction, the best dessert cooked up — all of these can earn the winner more booze. It makes mundane things far more interesting, and it turns average stories into legendary yarns.

I also find that the fancier the drink, the better the reaction from your fellow campers. Concocting a Cosmopolitan or igniting a shot of sambuca instantly warms up the group, generally because such swanky comforts seem to put people at ease in places unfamiliar to them. The simple act of having a glass of wine with dinner or a shot of brandy around the campfire makes everything a little more "civilized." Not to use alcohol as a crutch, but the more I drink out there, the less I notice being eaten alive by mosquitoes at dusk and the less I fear a bear wandering into camp.

PERFECT BUSH MARTINI

I never go jogging, it makes me spill my martini.

— George Burns

After a long day of portaging through a bug-infested bog or scrambling up a steep peak, there's no other way to wind down than to sip elegantly on what is commonly known by all "happy campers" as the Bush Martini.

Why not? The martini itself is said to have been created for a gold miner who wandered out of the wilderness and into a saloon in Martinez, California (1862). He wanted his empty bottle filled with something worth the weight of his small pouch of gold, and thought just plain whisky wouldn't cut it. So the bartender filled it with a concoction of spirits, plopped an olive in it, and named the drink after the town.

Most outdoor enthusiasts consider themselves far too complex for the common gin and vermouth cocktail and as many Bush Martini recipes have been created as there are reasons to drag yourself through the wilderness. Beginners usually go for the simple but effective pouring of equal parts gin and cherry-flavored Kool-Aid in an enamel coffee cup — shaken, not stirred, in a good-size water bottle. But the presentation is less than civilized. There's the classic Cosmopolitan — four parts vodka, two parts triple sec, two parts Crystal Lite Cranberry Breeze mix, and a squirt of lime juice. The ultimate, however, is the Blue Sky: an ounce of vodka, a quarter ounce of sweet vermouth, a quarter ounce of blue curaçao and, to finish, a garnish of three plump blueberries speared on a dried pine needle. Now that's the perfect Bush Martini.

The best part about drinking in the wilderness is that those who are connoisseurs of mixed drinks in the civilized world are less likely to harshly judge your creative efforts behind the backwoods bar (especially if you're getting low on spirits). The camping culture, when it comes to cocktails, is

Cheers! The author enjoys a classic Cosmopolitan in Quetico.

very experimental, at least in the group I travel with. We've treated our taste buds to some incredible drinks, and also mixed some oddballs that have come close to ruining our drinking habits forever.

Fire Starter

This drink came about by complete accident. My partner and I had limited alcohol left at the end of a long trip (a small quantity of peppermint schnapps and an equal amount of Southern Comfort). It was a miserable night, and after failing to get a fire started we decided to mix the booze we had left, swallow it down, and then just go to bed. The drink hit the spot more than we could have ever imagined and now it's one of our staples.

$\frac{1}{2}$ ounce Southern Comfort
$1\frac{1}{2}$ ounces peppermint schnapps

Pour schnapps into cup. Place a teaspoon just above the cup of schnapps, and slowly pour Southern Comfort onto the spoon so it stays as a separate layer on top of schnapps. Do not mix; it must be layered. Then ignite the Southern Comfort with a lighter or match and let it burn for 15 seconds before blowing it out and consuming it.

"What's the good of thirty millions when I ain't got room for more than a quart of cocktails a day? If I had a hundred-quart-cocktail thirst, it'd be different. But one quart – one measly little quart! Here I am, a thirty times over millionaire, slaving harder every day than any dozen men that work for me, and all I get is two meals that don't taste good, one bed, a quart of Martini, and a hundred and forty hair bridles to look at on the wall."

– Jack London, *Burning Daylight* (1910)

"I'll trade you some hooch for a full roll of toilet paper and a pair of dry socks." Ashley McBride, Kawartha Highlands Park.

Swamp Water

My wife made up this drink for a Mardi Gras party and it was such a big hit we packed it along on one of our trips. The name comes from what it looks like after it's mixed up — swamp water.

1 ounce vodka
splash of blue curaçao
1 package of orange drink mix

Shake orange drink mix up in a mixing container. Pour vodka and curaçao in cup, and then add mix to taste.

Nightcap Martini

The main ingredient is white crème de cacao, and the word "cacao" is French for cocoa. Having that name in the recipe alone makes it fitting for any camping trip.

2½ ounces gin
1 ounce white crème de cacao
½ ounce blue curaçao

Pour everything into a mixing container, shake, and then pour into mug.

Calm Before the Storm

This recipe is based on the well-known Hurricane Martini, but has a gentler twist to it, and makes a darn good warm-up before mixing a Hurricane.

1 ounce light rum
1 ounce dark rum
1 ounce vodka
1 ounce gin
1 ounce raspberry liqueur
1 ounce triple sec liqueur
3 ounces orange/tango Crystal Lite drink crystals
1 maraschino cherry or orange slices for garnish

Pour everything into a mixing container, shake gently and add maraschino cherry or orange slice for garnish. If mixed right, it should have a pink grapefruit color to it.

Hurricane

This is a darn good drink to have while you're huddled under the rain tarp, wondering if the storm brewing is so bad you'll soon see Dorothy and her little dog Toto go flying by.

1 ounce dark rum
splash of grenadine
4 ounces grapefruit Crystal Lite juice crystals
2 ounces orange/mango Crystal Lite juice crystals

Mix everything except grenadine, and then add enough grenadine until the drink turns red.

Algonquin Martini

I like this recipe simply because of the name. Algonquin is a well-known park in Ontario, Canada, and I canoe there regularly. The drink is more appropriate for car-campers because of the can of club soda needed. Of course, it might be titled after the Algonquin Hotel in New York, established in 1902, where the infamous $10,000 "Martini on the Rock" is made. Why the high price? At the bottom of the glass is a sparking diamond.

1½ ounce Canadian Club whisky
1 ounce dry vermouth
1 ounce pineapple juice
1 ounce of club soda

Pour whisky, vermouth and juice into a mixing container. Shake. Pour into mug and top with club soda.

Cinnamon Stick Martini

This is a good choice for after dinner and sitting around the fire. It's also one that seems to impress new campers who aren't used to fancy drinks. So be sure to include the cinnamon stick and garnish.

2 ounces rum
1 ounce Applejack
1 teaspoon cinnamon
1 cinnamon stick
apple slice for garnish

Blend rum, Applejack and cinnamon in a mixing container. Pour into mug, stir with cinnamon stick and add apple slice for garnish.

If you think the photo is funny, you should have seen the look on his mother's face when it was published in a major magazine. Ashley models a Blue Sky martini.

Hershey Squirt Martini

Another after-dinner drink to savor around the campfire and to impress any newbie to the group.

2 ounces vodka
1 ounce Godiva chocolate liqueur
1 ounce white crème de cacao
1 chocolate stick
shredded dark unsweetened chocolate

Pour all spirits into a mixing container, shake, and then pour into mug. Add chocolate stick and sprinkle shredded dark unsweetened chocolate on top.

Wake Up and Smell the Coffee Martini

This is a great recipe to have on a cold afternoon, especially when the weather is too bad for travel and you find yourself stuck under a tarp waiting for the rain to stop. Just make sure to measure the ingredients as precisely as you can to get the best taste.

2 ounces vodka
1 ounce dry vermouth
1 ounce Frangelico
6 coffee beans

Pour all spirits into a mixing container, shake, and then pour into mug. Add coffee beans for presentation.

Rob Roy Martini

John Macgregor's book A Thousand Miles in a Rob Roy Canoe, *published in 1866, spawned such a huge interest in recreational canoeing, the guy deserves a toast on your next trip. Here's a perfect recipe for the occasion.*

3 ounces Scotch
½ teaspoon dry vermouth
lemon twist for garnish

Pour all spirits into a mixing container, shake, and then pour into mug. Add garnish.

Jack London

Jack London, the notable writer and author of Call of the Wild, *was also famous for his love of the martini. Here's the drink to have while reading his classic story "To Build a Fire" out loud at the campfire.*

3 ounces currant vodka
1 ounce Dubonnet blanc
½ ounce maraschino liqueur
lemon twist

Pour all spirits into a mixing container, shake, and then pour into mug. Add garnish.

Summer Sun Martini

This is one of the best cocktails to have while relaxing around camp on a warm sunny day. The Frangelico gives it a unique taste but it could be easily replaced by the same amount of coffee-flavored vodka.

2 ounces vanilla-flavored vodka
1 ounce Frangelico
1 teaspoon peach schnapps
dried (or fresh) peach slice

Pour all spirits into a mixing container, shake, and then pour into mug. Add garnish.

Tea Time Martini

This recipe came about by mixing up what was left at the bottom of the booze barrel at the end of a long trip. The key ingredient was a bag of chamomile tea that no one had bothered brewing up.

2 ounces vodka
1 package of mixed ice tea drink crystals
1 bag of chamomile tea
1 tablespoon lemon juice
lemon wedge for garnish

Mix ice tea crystals with 32 ounces (1 L) of water, add lemon juice, let chamomile tea bag soak in ice tea and water for at least 15 minutes. Pour spirits into a mug and pour in ice tea mix. Add garnish.

Famous Martini Drinkers

- Kingsley Amis
- Sherwood Anderson
- Robert Benchley
- Humphrey Bogart
- George Burns
- George Bush Sr.
- James Carville
- Sir Winston Churchill
- Noel Coward

- W.C. Fields
- M.F.K. Fisher
- F. Scott Fitzgerald
- Ian Fleming
- Gerald Ford
- Jackie Gleason
- Dashiell Hammett
- Ernest Hemingway
- William Holden

- Herbert Hoover
- Jack London
- Dean Martin
- H.L. Mencken
- Richard Nixon
- Franklin Delano Roosevelt
- James Thurber
- Mae West
- E.B. White

THERE'S A BLACKFLY
IN MY CHARDONNAY

An old man turned ninety-eight
He won the lottery and died the next day
It's a blackfly in your Chardonnay
It's a death row pardon two minutes too late
And isn't it ironic... don't you think.

— Alanis Morissette, "Ironic"

"I think the darn fly drank half my wine." Andy Baxter, Killarney Park.

My wife and I have gone to desperate measures to minimize the weight and bulk in our packs for one simple reason — so we can pack more wine. This, of course, only equals out to a glass per night (we tend to do long trips) but the pleasure of sipping an Australian Pinot Grigio or a Beaujolais Superieur from France is worth it.

Storage has been very experimental through the years. Initially, since good wine came in bottles and bad wine came in boxes, we packed our wine in plastic drink containers such as Nalgene bottles. We even carried unused fuel containers. The system worked but we always had an empty container to lug around after the wine was gone. To reduce bulk we changed over to drinking tubes (Platypus Reservoir is our favorite brand). The container holds the contents of one bottle of wine and, with a durable zip-lock closing system, there's a good chance the wine won't leak. The inside of the container is also coated with a polyethylene lining that ensures there's no plastic taste.

Present-day box wines are also handy to pack along and the quality is far superior. You simply crush the container after you're done to minimize bulk. They're also more environmental; even if you recycle your wine bottle, the wine carton produces less greenhouse gas emissions overall. However, they do on occasion leak if you don't put the cap back on properly.

What's good for the cook can be good for the meal too. There's no better way to impress your camping companions than to add a dash of red wine to reconstituted spaghetti sauce or white wine to a white sauce poured over baked fish fillets. In fact, any meal that required water can be greatly enhanced by replacing about half the liquid with wine. The only negative is that any spirit heated for five minutes or more loses its alcohol content.

Wine can make an excellent base for marinade. I've soaked beef jerky and even tofu in a cup of red wine for the day before adding it to a meal and

Top-Rated Box Wines

Whites

Banrock Station Unwooded Chardonnay (Australia) *Crisp and fruity, this wine has citrus and stone fruit flavors.*

Three Thieves "Bandit" Pinot Grigio (California) *Light, crisp, and simple.*

Frisky Zebra Sauvignon Blanc 2006 (South Africa) *Definitely a frisky taste with a citrus flavor and a touch of gooseberry and grapefruit. It's not intense but has a slightly bitter rind finish.*

Reds

Banrock Station Shiraz (Australia) *Classic berry fruit and black pepper.*

Red Lips Syrah (France) *Juicy and ripe with flavors of blackberry, cherry, plum, and vanilla, and a surprising hit of tannin.*

Le Petit Sommelier Shiraz/Grenache (France) *A peppery spice of Shiraz, the fresh, juicy berry flavor of Grenache.*

no longer does it taste like cooked cardboard. And a tasty salad dressing can simply be made up by adding a teaspoon of powdered mustard and six tablespoons of olive oil to three teaspoons of white wine and a clove of crushed garlic. The best use of wine for cooking, however, is in a cheese fondue. Simply pour a tablespoon of olive oil in a pot and mix in two tablespoons of all-purpose flour. Then add the wine (one cup of a dry white works best). Bring everything to a boil, adding a handful or two of grated old cheddar cheese and mixing until the cheese melts and the concoction begins to bubble. Everything from bread to broccoli can be dipped.

HOT TODDIES

What hot toddies have in common with hot chocolate and tea and coffee is that you can warm your hands by wrapping them round your mug while you sip. But hot toddies are just that little bit better to savor around the campfire if you want the night to seem less chilled, stars somewhat brighter and friends more pleasant to be with. And, if you dare, they also make the morning air less frosty.

The name "hot toddy" itself originated in Scotland, and is said to have come via a member of the British East India Company who extracted toddy, the fermented juice of a particular species of palm tree. A different reference to the drink, however, is to "kettles full of Todian spring" in Allan Ramsay's poem *The Morning Interview,* published in 1721, in which Todian refers to Tod's Well, which supplied Edinburgh with water.

The alcohol used in a hot toddy is traditionally brandy, rum or whisky. To that you can add either tea, coffee, hot chocolate, hot water or hot lemonade. Sweeteners such as honey, sugar or syrup are then added. Anything added after that — such as cinnamon sticks or cloves — allows you to call the recipe your own. Here are a few of my favorites.

Ginger Snap Toddy

1 ounce whisky
¼ cup apple cider vinegar
¼ cup maple syrup
1 tablespoon molasses
1 teaspoon finely grated fresh ginger

Add liquid ingredients to a pot and bring to a boil. Simmer for 3–5 minutes and then let steep for another 15 minutes. Grate ginger (skin and all) on top.

African Delight

1 ounce brandy
1 tablespoon honey
1 cup hot water
1 Rooibos herbal tea bag
lemon wedge

Coat bottom of camp mug with honey then add brandy, juice of the lemon slice. Boil water and steep tea bag for 5–7 minutes. Pour hot tea into mug.

Chocolate Buzz

1 ounce Irish Cream
¼ cup instant espresso powder
6 ounces hot water
¼ teaspoon ground cinnamon
1 chunk of semisweet chocolate

Add espresso, Irish Cream and ground cinnamon to the boiled water in a camp mug and grate chunk of chocolate on top.

SINGLE MALT SCOTCH WHISKY

Too much of anything is bad, but too much of good whiskey is barely enough.

— Mark Twain

There are campers out there who truly believe that the only spirit that should be packed along on a trip is a single malt whisky. I'm not talking about brands like Yukon Jack, which is a honey-based liqueur labeled "the black sheep of the Canadian whiskys," or something like Crown Royal, which is a rye whisky. I'm talking about a barley malt Scotch whisky distilled from barley and made in Scotland.

Becoming a Scotch snob isn't such a bad idea on the trip. After all, a little bit goes a long way. Tradition states that only two ounces after dinner, preferably with a cigar, is all that's required on trip. The only bulky part is the container holding it and the glass you're drinking from. It's a sin supposedly to use anything but glass. Scotch stored in a Nalgene and sipped from an enamel camp mug is definitely frowned upon.

To make it last a little longer, it's quite acceptable to add a bit of water — but only the best water obtainable. Some experts claim you add the Scotch to the water and some say it's the other way around. I believe that adding water to the Scotch helps bring out the flavor.

Essential Grains

The word "whisky" is from the Gaelic *uisgebeatha*, or "water of life" and is technically an alcoholic liquor made by distillation of a fermented starch compound (usually grain). The act of fermenting grain dates as far back as the 7th century AD by the Chinese, five centuries before the Europeans got around to it. But Scotland is best known for developing its diverse taste.

Scotch can be peaty and rich, light and smooth, or somewhere in between. It seems to me that anything sounding Anglo Saxon and aged 10 to 18 years old is acceptable for camping trips. Among my camping mates, brands from the Isle of Islay, such as 16-year old Lagavulin, 10-year-old Ardbeg, 17-year-old Bowmore, 18-year-old Caol lla or 10-year-old Laphroaig, are legendary. Ten-year-old Talisker from the Isle of Skye is a great choice. And a friend, author Michael Peake, tells me Highland Park from Orkney Islands, northern Scotland, is "the most economical libation in its class and the source of many Hudson Bay Company employees."

The water was not fit to drink. To make it palatable, we had to add whisky. By diligent effort, I learnt to like it.

— Sir Winston Churchill

IRISH CAMP COFFEE

It's getting tougher to get up in the morning on camping trips. I hate to admit it, but my father was right. He always told me that one day I would regret spending most of my time sleeping on the cold ground. Arthritis runs in our family and now that I am over the age of forty and still spending a good deal of time outdoors, my poor joints ache every morning as I awake in the tent. I'd rather suffer in pain than give up my time camping. The thing that helps me get up and ease into the day is the thought of that first cup of morning camp coffee.

Yes, I realize there are other substitutes; pain killers such as Advil or Tylenol come to mind. But for now I'm most motivated by the simple prospect of pouring a hot cup of java, inhaling the fragrant steam, anointing the dark brew with a dash of Irish Cream liqueur, and enjoying that first gulp of the day.

The coffee I brew up in the morning, however, is not just any coffee. It's true grit camp coffee, real grounds-and-water-in-the-pot coffee. I bring water to a rolling boil, take it off the heat source, dump in one generous tablespoon of coffee grounds per cup of water, and let it steep (covered) alongside the campfire for approximately five to ten minutes. To settle the grounds, tap a spoon on the side of the pot 3 to 5 times.

The most crucial element of brewing true grit is to never let the coffee boil once you've taken it off the heat source. Old-timers used to say that boiled coffee tastes like rotten shoe leather, and they're right! The reason for the bad taste of boiled coffee is in the bitter tannic acid and flavoring oils it contains. The tasty oils are released at 205° F (86° C), just below boiling point. The bitter acids, however, are released right at or just above boiling pot.

Another important factor is how to settle the grounds before serving the coffee. Some people throw pieces of eggshell or toss in a few round pebbles. I've even witnessed campers take hold of the wire handle on the pot, swing it with the speed of an aircraft propeller, and have complete faith in centrifugal force. This suicidal action will pull the grounds to the bottom of the pot — guaranteed. I merely tap the side of the pot with a knife or spoon and then make sure to offer the first and last cup of coffee to someone else in the group.

A drop of Irish Cream in the morning coffee is a great way to start the day.

GETTING CLOSE TO WILDLIFE — BUT NOT TOO CLOSE!

Whenever you observe an animal closely, you feel as if a human being sitting inside were making fun of you.

— Elias Canetti

I N HIS FILM *WATERWALKER,* BILL MASON, FAMED CANOEIST and filmmaker, says: "Nature films often give the impression that the country is running alive with animals. Well, I'll tell you right now, it's a lie. I'll canoe a whole summer and see one, two moose, maybe a bear if I'm lucky…. It's a really big deal to see an animal."

I have to say, he's right. I've traveled for days and seen as little as a chipmunk. That's why you should celebrate when you actually do see something special, especially big game such as a moose or bear. Those moments can be darn exciting.

It may seem that the best way to view wildlife is to drive down a back road and hope for the best; surprisingly, the method makes a lot of sense. I know if you're looking for moose in Algonquin Park near where I live, it's pretty much a given you're more likely to see one on the roadside driving into the park than you are in the interior. But there's a reason for that. The moose hanging around the roadside have become so accustomed to people that they seem to even stop to pose for a photo when visitors exit their vehicles for a photo shoot.

Looking for wildlife along roadsides, however, severely limits the types of species you'll come across. After all, seeing an animal is only half the fun;

Andy tries to get better reception for the satellite phone.

seeing an animal acting out in its own natural environment is far more rewarding.

Once on a long canoe trip in Ontario's Quetico park my canoe companion and I were lucky enough to come upon a wolf preying on a raven when we rounded a bend in a creek. Andy and I heard the commotion first — two ravens were screaming uncontrollably — and we slowed the progress of the canoe just before the crook in the waterway. As we drifted around the corner, we saw a large, beige timber wolf in the middle of snatching on to one raven's wing while the other bird repeatedly dive-bombed the prowler. The wind wasn't in our favor, but the wolf was so preoccupied with both ravens that we were able to float close to the action. It was like watching a nature documentary unfolding right in front of us — until I decided to reach for my camera. Just one slight movement was all it took for the wolf to look up, spot us only a couple of canoe-lengths away, and then give up on the two birds to escape into the thick brush. The wounded bird took refuge halfway up an alder patch alongside the creek while his buddy continued to harass the wolf in the backwoods. It was obvious that the wolf was patiently waiting for us to continue on. So we did just that, and a few minutes downstream Andy and I noticed that only one raven was now calling out. I guess the wolf got its meal for the day, and we got one of the best wildlife moments of our life.

So, take note and get off the beaten path. And be prepared to take a good photograph. It's difficult but there's nothing better than having a snapshot of some wild beast displayed on your office desk, or better yet on your screensaver. It becomes a constant reminder of how wild the landscape was you traveled through and, more important, how wild it remains — waiting for you to return.

COMMON CAMP CRITTERS

Hunters will tell you that a moose is a wily and ferocious forest creature. Nonsense. A moose is a cow drawn by a three-year-old.
— Bill Bryson, *A Walk in the Woods* (1997)

One of the best places to spot wildlife while traveling through the interior is right at your own campsite. Some come in to camp because curiosity has finally gotten the better of them. Others are just passing through and try to ignore that you've taken over their turf. And some even sneak in to steal a bit of food. Whatever the case, it's great to have them visit. Keep your eyes open for some of my favorite camp regulars — these are native to the typical canoe country of the Precambrian Shield.

A lovesick moose blocked our path in Algonquin Park.

Moose

A bull moose, especially during rutting season, is more apt to be a problem in camp than a bear. I've woke up in the middle of the night a few times to discover a moose standing over the tent, wondering if it should jump over the guy ropes or just crash straight through, trampling me inside. There was the time when I had to set up camp directly on a portage. It was a bad idea but it was late and I simply couldn't go any further. Luckily the moose walked around me, taking one of my socks with it. I haven't a clue why it took my sock but wasn't about to argue at the time.

Lovesick moose are the worst to deal with. Usually the animal is quite calm and gentle. However, during the fall rut (late September to early October), males become extremely aggressive and unpredictable. Basically, they get so excited about the mating ritual that they sometimes mistake large objects for female moose. For this reason sex-mad bulls have been known to attack vehicles, charge trains, and even tree innocent campers.

The male's aggression lets up the moment its antlers drop off sometime in December. By spring, though, it begins its search for salt, which it needs to help develop a good rack, and the cycle soon begins all over again.

Red Squirrel

Have you ever found yourself lying snug inside your sleeping bag, waiting for the first rays of sun to rise before you crawl out to meet the day, when all of a sudden the roof of the tent is bombarded by a bunch of pine cones? Then, the moment you unzip your tent door to see if the sky is falling or not, you hear the noisy chatter of a red squirrel and then get struck right on the noggin with a resin-soaked cone?

Don't take the assault personally. The main reason the squirrel is clipping cones from the treetops is to gather enough for winter storage; something it takes very seriously. By the end of the season it will have cached literally thousands of cones (they average 100 per day), stashing them in stumps, hollow logs, underground, or anywhere there's shade and the cones won't dry up and disperse their seeds.

The reason for the irritable scolding it gives you is that it just doesn't like being interrupted. The squirrel is definitely a high-energy, aggressive rodent that gets extremely annoyed with intruders in its territory. It is well known for fighting off gray jays, the larger gray squirrel, owls, and even the odd camper.

The red squirrel is not fixed on eating seeds alone. In fact, it's overtly carnivorous, adding mice, large insects, bird's eggs, and fledglings to its diet. It also has a taste for mushrooms and will hang them out on tree limbs to dry. The poisons contained in the mushrooms have little effect on the rodent, but it's thought that trappers who went "squirrelly" had actually dined on too many mushroom-eating squirrels.

Chipmunk

Native legend tells of a time when it was undecided if the earth would be covered in complete darkness or continuous light. The decision was left to two of the forest animals: the bear, fighting for night, and the chipmunk battling for day.

Most of the animals placed their bet on the bear, thinking the bruin's strength and size would overpower the tiny chipmunk's. But when the struggle began, the quick and agile rodent easily outmaneuvered the awkward bear. Eventually, however, the bear managed to trap the chipmunk under its massive paw and it looked as if darkness would soon cover the earth forever. Luckily, at the last minute, the spry chipmunk squeezed its slender body out from under the bruin's grasp. The battle ended in a tie, allowing the earth to have both day and night, and to this day the chipmunk bears the five brownish-black scars across its back to remind everyone of the fight between darkness and light.

Today the chipmunk's mythic war wounds come in handy for keeping it camouflaged from its aerial predators, the five stripes blending in with the

The chipmunk was cute, that is, until it stole half my stash of nuts.

dark shadows of twigs and plants. Chipmunks spend a lot of their time underground constructing an elaborate system of tunnels, complete with food storage areas and escape hatches. It's almost impossible to locate the main entrance of the burrow since the rodent goes out of its way to rid the area of any trace of the excavated dirt, stuffing it in its cheek pouches and spreading it evenly across the forest floor.

If you happen to spot a chipmunk chasing another of its kind through the campsite, with its tail jerking and making loud chirping noises, it's most likely due to the fact that the other chipmunk has just robbed it of its food cache. Chipmunks are solitary creatures and only pair up to mate. They devote most of their time to gathering and storing food underground since the rodent does not truly hibernate. Its metabolism is only reduced during cold snaps and the chipmunk will actually awaken periodically during winter to munch on its food supply.

Porcupine

The first time I heard a porcupine's mating call, it scared me silly. The beast was having sex directly beside my tent when it let out an eerie cry, sounding like the wail of a banshee. I had no idea what was making the noise at the time and only realized it was a porcupine when I slapped the side of the tent to scare the monster away and it released a few hundred quills into the nylon fly.

When morning came, I slowly crept out of the tent and there was the porcupine, resting comfortably high up in a pine tree. And below the tree was my wooden paddle, its shaft chewed to pieces. It was attracted to my salty sweat, which had collected on the paddle. I'd seen porcupines chew on wood before. Toilet seats in the outhouse are a favorite snack and so are plywood portage signs since they contain tasty glue. But I never thought I'd have my paddle munched on. I was glad my spare was made of plastic.

I wanted to get even, but the idea of getting stuck with a few dozen quills made me rethink getting revenge. The porcupine doesn't actually shoot its quills (of which there are over 30,000). If you do approach too closely, however, it will raise the quills up and attempt to swat you with its tail where the majority of them are. If you do get hit, it's more than a simple pin prick; the quill is tipped with hundreds of tiny barbs and each time your muscle contracts it works deeper and deeper beneath the skin. Dogs and other animals who have come face to tail with a porcupine have been known to die by a single quill working its way through the brain, slowly driving it mad.

Raccoon

Raccoons are notorious camp robbers and more than one camper has had to deal with their persistence in stealing food scraps from right under their nose. They're smart, smarter than their close cousin the bear, and when cornered can be extremely vicious. I once attempted to scare off a family of raccoons who were in the midst of tearing off the rubber seal on my truck cab to get at my cooler. I lost the battle and found myself standing on top of the picnic table, surrounded with half-a-dozen hissing and snapping raccoons when the park ranger arrived to see what all the fuss was about.

Raccoons are nocturnal and have adapted to rummaging for food just by feel. With thousands of nerve endings on their hands they can easily sense the presence of food before seeing it, which is why they are so successful opening up camp coolers and garbage cans. It's also believed that water actually enhances their sense of touch and that is why they will head off to wash their food in a nearby stream.

Loon

The loon's primeval call, made up of a series of wails and yodels, is a true symbol of the north country, a sound that will definitely lull you to sleep at night and awaken you early enough to witness the morning mist burning off the lake.

Remarkably, the song itself has a great number of meanings, ranging from an expression of alarm to a simple hello. The most distinctive yodel, the one that's usually heard at night while you lie snug inside your sleeping bag, comes from separate males, all which have their own distinct sound, talking to one another from lake to lake. It's also the male of the species that you see running across the surface of the lake, widely flapping its wings and yodeling uncontrollably. It's a sure sign of aggression and is used to either chase off another rival male or to protect its young from a possible predator.

Loons prefer lakes that are deep enough to dive for fish and long enough to provide a decent runway for taking off. The bone structure of the loon is not hollow like most water birds. It has a solid bone structure, which allows it to sink rapidly to depths of 200 feet (60 m) and allows it lie just beneath the surface of the water, catching a quick breath before submerging again and leaving you wondering where on earth it has gone. However, the loon's extra weight also makes it extremely difficult for it to take off and less than graceful when on land. The legs are so far back on its body that it can

The loon is truly the symbol of the north.

hardly stand, let alone run if needed. For this reason it's rare to see a loon on land, and if it is approached while sitting on its nest the bird will most likely panic and may even abandon her nest completely.

Keep an eye out for a decline in loon populations on the lakes you visit on a regular basis. Wave action from motorboats and jet skis disturbs nests, and toxic pollutants in the water and acid rain are starving them out.

Common Merganser

This diving duck is usually spotted swimming close to shore with its half-dozen or more goslings waddling close behind. Not all the young birds came from the parent, however. The merganser has a habit of adopting as many goslings as possible to help it corral minnows along the shoreline. The goslings will form a half V and each bird will take turns snatching up the minnows caught between the line of birds and the shoreline.

It's the female merganser that has a distinctive, bright, chestnut-colored head and crest, while the male has a white breast, a dark glossy head, and lacks the female's breast. Don't mistake the common merganser with the more northern red-breasted merganser. The male red-breasted has a crest and a streaked breast. The female's crest is dull in color and has a full, pale, white-colored collar and breast. Also, the common merganser is like the wood duck and nests in the hollows of dead trees.

Canoeists claim that mergansers have the amazing ability to float care-free down a raging rapid and come out at the end without a scratch. However, it's best to scout the rapid on your own rather than follow a duck.

Great Blue Heron

In midsummer great blue herons are loners and are usually found searching the shallows adjacent to your campsite for fish and frogs. The birds are amazing to watch as they stand frozen in the water, waiting for their prey to come to them. Then, with amazing accuracy, they lash out with their long, sharp bills spearing the unsuspecting dinner and swallowing it whole.

In flight the great blue heron will usually squawk or croak. Look for the long skinny legs dragging behind the tail and the dropping neck (a sandhill crane's neck stays outstretched when flying).

Early spring is the only time these large crane-like birds congregate, nesting in large, elaborate stick structures called rookeries. This is also when the heron is most vulnerable. As a defensive strategy, however, they're known for whitewashing or vomiting on any predator attempting to climb up after them. In close quarters the heron will even jab its javelin-like bill, aiming straight for its enemy's eyes.

The rookeries themselves are difficult to find, and if you happen to come across a nesting area it's best to keep well away. Herons are notorious for abandoning their young at the slightest cause for alarm.

Gray Jay

I swear that gray jays, those fluffy gray-feathered birds with a white forehead and collar, come equipped with some type of homing device locked on to soft-hearted camp cooks. They're legendary for their bold approach at pan-handling food scraps, and based on my past experience with them I can tell you they prefer greasy bacon over bannock any day.

There are many names given to the bird. Ornithologists still insist on calling it the Canada Jay. But true northerners have named the bird "camp robber." I've also heard it called "whiskeyjack." It's not that the bird has a taste for liquor. The term is derived from the Algonkian word "Wisakedjak" used to denote a trickster — a supernatural shape-shifting spirit that loves to play pranks on campers.

Gray jays are close cousins to the blue jay. But rather than migrate south in winter, they are able to survive the cold months by storing food caches all summer. Watch them the next time they steal a bit of food from you. They'll first coat it with saliva, which acts as a preservative, and then stuff the food behind a piece of bark or tree moss.

The Creature from the Black Lagoon

Most have heard of Scotland's Loch Ness Monster; but you may not have heard of these mysterious water creatures.

- **Igopogo** is thought to haunt the depths of Canada's Lake Simcoe, in south-central Ontario. Residents of the local town Beaverton called the creature Beaverton Bessie, while those of another nearby town, Kempenfelt Bay, call it Kempenfelt Kelly. Main sightings occurred in 1952 and 1963, followed by a sonar recording in 1983 and a video tape of a "seal-like animal measuring 70 feet long, with a distinct dog or horse-like face, dorsal fine and fish-like tail" in 1991.

- **Ogopogo** is a legendary creature lurking in the waters of British Columbia's Okanagan Lake. There have been countless sightings and stories about its existence. The name is immortalized in a ditty: "His mother was an earwig, his father was a whale, a little bit of head and hardly any tail . . . and Ogopogo was his name."

- **Champ** is a serpent-like creature 15 to 25 feet (5–8 m) long, at home in Lake Champlain in northeast New York.

- The **Altamaha-ha** haunts the Altamaha River near Darien, Georgia. It's been sighted countless times, mostly by fishermen, since the 1960s.

- **Memphre** lives in Lake Memphremagog, which straddles the American-Canadian border just east of Montreal. The earliest sighting of the serpent creature goes back to 1847.

"Looks like moose poop to me — I hope." The author discovers fresh scat behind his tent in Algonquin Park.

WHO POOPED BEHIND MY TENT?

Nature programs are deceiving. They make it look as if animal sightings are commonplace out there. Reality check. They're not. In fact, the closest you might come to knowing if an animal walked into camp is to catch a glimpse of the poop it left behind your tent during the night. You may not think of this as one of the highlights of your camping trip, but once you learn the art of scatology, you will be better able to tell tall tales of the animal who crept behind your tent in the night.

Black and Grizzly Bear

This is one you definitely want to know how to recognize, because if you spot bear poop on the campsite you'll want to move to another campsite. Size, color and shape varies due to diet of the bear but generally it is "log" shaped, more black than brown, averages 5 cm (2 in) and usually contains a number of undigested seeds — think of human waste the morning after a corn roast. And you'd think the only difference between black and grizzly bear scat is size — and that the larger would belong to a grizzly bear. Truth be known, however, almost 60 percent of grizzly bear scat found was smaller than black bear. Who knew?

Moose

Large piles of brown capsule-shaped pellets in winter and less distinct olive-colored piles in summer, similar to lumpy cow-patties (they get the trots from eating too much fresh greenery). When dried they can be burned in the campfire to replicate a spruce-scented incense.

White-tail Deer

Pellets are oval shaped, thinner and smaller than those of moose. In spring they're light brownish-black and clumped together; in summer they're more black; and winter they look more like large brown jelly beans.

Cougar

Cougar scat is segmented, just under an inch long, with the ends rounded more than canine scat, and maybe a few tufts of hair mixed in with it. However, like all cats, cougars like to scratch a bit of dirt on top of their poop and top it off with a sprinkle or two of urine, so it is rarely found in the open. It's a territorial thing. To help you with the analysis, just remember back when you played in the sand box as a kid and dug up a round, segmented piece of clay. It wasn't clay. It was cat poop. Cougar poop looks the same but is bigger, and definitely smellier.

Wolf

Measures approximately 4 inches (10 cm) and looks pretty much like dog poop at first glance, but upon close examination you'll see it's made up of bone chips and mats of fur, tapered at one end, and held together with mucus.

River Otter

The wet and clumpy poops of otters have to be some of the oddest and most intriguing out there, mainly because of the revealing pile of non-digested material it leaves behind: reddish external skeletons of crayfish, jagged fish bones (that's gotta hurt), and lots of fish scales. You have to wonder if its diet is working for it at all. Fish scales are even so intact that biologists collect them, age them and determine the levels of PCBs the otters were digesting.

Owl and hawk pellets (cough pellets or castings) are sometimes mistaken for animal scat but are actually the undigested remains of what the birds have eaten and regurgitated from their gizzards. The pellets are usually found near roosting sites, which means if you look up from the glob of hair, bones, claws, and beaks you might catch sight of the bird that just spat it out.

LYNX ENCOUNTER

How do you tell the difference between a lynx and a bobcat? You yell out "Hey, Bob!" If he turns around, you know it's a bobcat.

— Alana Callan

We should have realized that a portage named after Lucifer wouldn't be easy. It's not as if we weren't warned. Other canoeists had cautioned me and my wife, Alana, before the trip. But we've listened to so many paddlers exaggerate the difficulty of particular canoe routes that we were more than skeptical about the rumors of this particular trail. How could a portage begin by going up a sheer cliff? When we arrived at the take-out, however, and saw an arrow spray-painted on a tree, pointing straight up a giant slab of granite, we knew the warnings were well justified.

Our plan was to first haul our gear and canoe up the almost vertical section of the trail. Once we had everything up on the summit, Alana and I would then double-carry over what remained — a somewhat level but extremely rugged path that worked through a steep-walled ravine for approximately a kilometer. It sounded reasonable. But on any regular portage, walking with at least half your body weight strapped to your back is no easy task. Pulling yourself up a 30-degree slope, with loose rocks and fallen trees littering the path, that's just silly.

Somehow we managed to get the first two packs up. Even our hyper springer spaniel, Bailey, coped with lugging her ten pounds of dog kibble to the top. On the second trip, Alana had to deal with the largest of our packs, which she ended up dragging most of the way, and I had the darn canoe to carry.

At first I cursed a lot, hoping the profanity would give me some type of superhuman strength to help me along. But I finally had to give in about halfway. At this point the bow of the canoe was continuously ramming into the trail in front of me. Any forward motion became impossible and I had to resort to winching the canoe uphill by looping a rope around a solid tree at the top of the rise.

Bailey took a less cerebral approach. You may have heard that springer spaniels are hyper. Well…she's beyond that. When it comes to portaging, she just basically wants the ordeal over as quickly as possible so she can go back to snoozing in the canoe. I've given up trying to leash her while on the trail, which is why we only take her on remote trips where there's little chance of meeting up with another person carrying across the portage. The dog's routine is simple — jump out of the canoe as we approach the take-out, wait impatiently as I lash her pack on, and then sprint across to the put-in to take in a relaxing swim while waiting for us to catch up. This dog definitely has an attitude.

An hour later Alana and I had successfully dragged everything up to the summit and then mentally prepared ourselves for what remained — a rocky ravine littered with giant boulders and deep crevices. Then, sometime between Alana doing a face-plant after twisting an ankle in a narrow crack in the rock and me crunching my crotch while trying to straddle a giant boulder, we heard Bailey whimpering ahead of us. I helped Alana up first, then jogged ahead to see what was up with poor Bailey. Around the second bend in the trail I witnessed a very unusual sight; Bailey was standing in the middle of the trail, whimpering even louder than before and trembling uncontrollably, while a few feet away a wild lynx, positioned in a classic predatory position, was slowly moving in for the kill.

I had never seen a lynx before, which is my excuse for why my first reaction was to unpack my camera rather try to rescue my dog. Poor Bailey, loaded down with her week's ration of kibble, didn't stand a chance of escaping the stalking cat. When the dog saw me trying to snap a picture of her assailant, she gave me a look that made me glad dogs can't talk — or swear. Guilt ridden, I dropped the camera and chased off the lynx with a paddle.

We finished the portage shortly after, but I still don't have a photo of a lynx, and Bailey's been afraid of the neighbors' cat ever since.

Bailey still wasn't talking to me a full day after the lynx incident.

Who ever told you bears are scary? It's the moose you should worry about.

RUNNING WITH THE MOOSE IN NORTHERN ONTARIO

I stood my ground when the moose initially started to charge, not believing it was a real threat. When it was only a few meters away, and changing its gait from a gallop to an all-out sprint, I suddenly changed my tune. I ran my ass off, making a beeline back to the truck.

What was I thinking? If I had come across the same animal while out on a trip and not by the side of the highway, I would have admired it from a distance, not blindly walked up to it snapping photos as if it was a supermodel.

A few seconds into the chase I realized that my days of the high school running club were far behind me, but the moose wasn't. He was closing in and the only thing to do was to start zig-zagging in hopes of confusing him.

It was the blast of a logging truck's horn that saved me in the end. Not my buddy Andy. He was too busy laughing uncontrollably and trying to figure out how to turn his video camera on. The moose jolted with the sound of the horn, zigged when I zagged, and gave up the chase as quickly as it started.

I'm an idiot. I really am. I'm quite a safety fanatic while out on a trip. It's a philosophy that's kept me alive many times out there. There are times, however, such as the last moment of the trip, when I find myself forgetting

How to Find More Wildlife

- Water sources (streams, ponds, wetlands, lakeshores) are the best places to hang out and wait for wildlife.

- Places where two different habitats collide act as travel corridors for many wildlife species (i.e., edges of fields and woodlots) and also become great places to spot various species.

- Dawn and dusk, especially the first and last hour, are when most species become more active and are therefore the best times to search them out.

- Sitting still for long periods of time, moving your eyes but not your head, is not easy for a lot of people nowadays but it's still the best way to see anything. Animals can detect your slightest movement.

- Stationed in higher ground and using binoculars or a spotting scope may be easier than sitting still exactly where you think the animals will show up.

- Blend in with your environment and camouflage yourself. Wear drab, natural colors.

- Don't wear scented deodorant, perfume or cologne.

- Cover or remove any objects that might reflect light from the sun.

- Avoid "creeping" up since most species can detect your nervous behavior. Relax and act naturally as possible. An animal will sense your presence far quicker than actually seeing you.

- Use rocks, trees and bushes to hide behind.

- Follow hedgerows rather than walk directly across an open field if you have to get closer.

- Avoid walking across hilltops and ridges where you will be easily spotted.

- Move slowly and quietly with no sudden movements.

- Leave the dog at home.

- To catch the attention of predator, and some prey species, try mimicking the sound of a wounded animal. Species such as otter or birds of prey will come and check things out.

- Look for tracks, scat or things like dens or nests.

- Stop every now and then, lie on the ground, and look up into the forest canopy; you'll be surprised by what's up there and what you're missing by simply walking by it.

- Listen for guardian birds such as ravens or blue jays calling out; they're usually pestering some other species.

- Make use of all your senses; fox pee smells like mild skunk spray; an alarmed deer will snort.

- Learn as much as you can about the species you are searching for.

all those over-the-top security measures, as if being reconnected with civilization makes it all okay again. Who am I kidding?

Before the moose attack, my regular canoe companion Andy Baxter and I, partnering up with Bill and Anne Ostrom, had spent two full weeks paddling a remote river in the far north (Kopka), a river that's challenging enough in normal conditions but was in high flood water during our trip. It was the most testing route I've ever done. Nothing bad happened, though. We played safe, excessively safe, actually. We scouted every rapid before running it. We hunkered down during a windstorm rather than take a chance surfing waves out on the big lakes en route. We encountered a total of ten bears and gave them all a wide berth (and our full respect). We even used safety harnesses while portaging an incredibly steep portage around Kopka Falls. We were the poster paddlers for safe canoe tripping.

I happened upon the moose feeding along the road side not long after Andy and I started the drive home. Andy and I hadn't seen a moose all trip, so I pulled over to take a picture. I suddenly transformed from Safety Boy to idiot tourist.

And what happened to the moose? He went back into the woods where it was safe, probably wondering how humans survive the real world, let alone a couple of weeks paddling in the wilderness.

Seconds before the charge.

CATCHING A TROUT ON A FLY

It is not a fish until it is on the bank.

— Irish proverb

In my family, there was no clear division between religion and fly fishing.

— Norman Maclean, *A River Runs Through It*, 1976

There's a fine line between fishing and standing on the shore like an idiot.

— Steven Wright

My poor nephew Todd; every Christmas he tells his stories of the past season's angling trips. The problem is, they're always about catching big bass or pike and I always rudely interrupt him halfway through by blurting out "So when are you going to catch a real fish?"

My father brought me up in a traditional sense — to always work hard, be honest to others, and know that the only worthwhile fish to catch is a trout. He also added that if you hook a trout with a fly, then all the better. Yes, bass or pike fishing is a lot of fun. But the species in no way represents, at least to me, the essence of true wilderness. A speckle trout, or what some call a "brookie," clearly defines it. The moment water becomes tainted or a road creates easy access, then the trout simply disappear, along with what they represent.

When I was a child, the act of fishing was my doorway to time spent outdoors. Even at a young age I knew that actually catching the fish was anticlimactic. The exciting part was trying to catch a fish, and the more difficult the species was to catch then the more solid the memory of the event and the more respect you gave to the species itself. Trout were always the hardest species to angle for.

My early years were spent just dangling a worm in a local creek. It wasn't until my preteens my father took me to cast a small spinner in a bona-fide trout stream with deep pools and oxygen-rich rapids. On my sixteenth birthday my father gave me a fly rod. To be honest, though, it wasn't until I reached the age of twenty-one I gave the art of fly-fishing a decent try.

I chose to go alone. The reason was innocent enough. It wasn't as if I didn't want anyone to see how incompetent I was. I was okay with that. I just didn't want anyone to think me a fishing snob when I obviously wasn't. That was for the guys clad in hip waders and floppy fedoras. I was wearing sneakers and a baseball cap. The movie *A River Runs Through It* hadn't been released yet but what was known as the Zen of fly-fishing was an active trend at the time.

And it's a good thing I had privacy too. My first attempt at moving the floating line back and forth through the air was totally embarrassing, with it whirling out of control around my head and the fly catching up on tree branches more often than not. If anyone were around they would have been hooked for sure. But I persisted, believing the more difficult the method, the bigger the trophy trout would be.

By the end of the practice run I was beginning to get the hang of it. Fly-fishing is a lot like golf. The more you try, the worse you get. But the moment you give up and don't really care if you strike the darn ball or not, you get a hole-in-one. By then you've figured out the groove. Timing and feel are the two crucial elements. The line is flung behind you and if you abruptly stop the rod at the appropriate moment, it just feels right. The line straightens out and you sense a slight tug of the tension that travels back down to your grip. It's at this particular moment you initiate the forward cast — making the fly land on the water the way nature intended it.

Just recently I talked about that first time fly-fishing with my nephew. It was at my father's funeral. Todd had been away fishing in northern Canada and came home for the service. After spinning a few tales, trying to make light of the situation at hand, Todd asked if he could place something in my father's casket. I said "yes" and added that he'd appreciate the gesture from his nephew.

It was a trout fly Todd gave my father, not a bass jig or pike spoon. We hugged after he had said his prayers and I whispered, "I guess you went on a real fishing trip while you were in the north." Todd smiled and quite enthusiastically replied, "I caught speckles the size of champagne bottles, Uncle Kevin, it was fantastic." My nephew had made good use of the gift my father gave him for his birthday before he died — it was a fly rod.

The Art of Fly-Fishing

Fly-fishing in moving water is a slightly bigger challenge than on the calm waters of a small pond. Attention must be given to what the experts call "mending the line." This is the practice of making sure the line always floats upstream of the fly.

Where there's a current the heavy line will always have a tendency to let itself be tugged all over the place, letting the fly in return swim sideways — something a bug never does.

To make the presentation of the fly as natural as possible, don't rush to reel it in. Let the fly drift with the current; keep the drag free and you'll soon grab the attention of the fish below.

A bass or a pike may be fun to catch but a trout is a real fish and nothing else compares.

9

WATCHING THE WEATHER

Weather is a great metaphor for life — sometimes it's good, sometimes it's bad, and there's nothing much you can do about it but carry an umbrella.

— Pepper Giardino

WEATHER MAKES A GOOD CONVERSATION STARTER WHEN you're trying to pass the time back in the civilized world, but while camping out in the elements, talking about the weather becomes a pure obsession. Maybe it's because of a closer connection with nature, a love affair with perfect sunsets and sunrises, and the chance to actually see the weather coming before it hits, or maybe it's because your fear of being washed away during a flash flood or getting struck by lightening is greatly heightened. Whatever the reason, you find yourself basically gazing up into the heavens a good deal of the time.

I think campers can be thankful that there's no continual weather report to monitor. They can also be thankful that weather can't and most likely will never be controlled by science and technology. And they can thank their lucky stars that not all days out there are full of sunshine and moderate temperatures. Variety is, after all, the spice of life.

Changing weather definitely makes things interesting while on a trip. It makes you and your group come together in an attempt to make important decisions. Important questions are asked. Should you paddle across an open bay before an approaching storm hits or wait until it passes? Should you pack your raingear on top of your pack even though the sun is shining during the breakfast hour? After the decisions are made and the ordeal is over, a

The calm before the storm on Lake Superior's North Shore.

bond is created that can never be broken. Group dynamics are surely heightened and many times I've seen friends become friendlier and adversaries become brutal enemies.

During one particular Algonquin trip a group of us who had paddled together since high school found ourselves windbound on the eastern shore of a large lake. Ice had just melted a week before our trip and the water was unquestionably hypothermic. The problem was, we were behind schedule and if we failed to get off that lake in the next hour or so our group would never have a chance to get back to the take-out at the designated time.

One member insisted we continue on and another insisted we didn't. The rest of us were unsure and kept quiet while the rivals battled it out. Eventually the decision was made to stay put. But that incident, occurring over twelve years ago, made a lasting impression. The two who argued haven't spoken since and by the next season the entire group had disbanded.

On a separate trip, however, reactions to a similar predicament were totally opposite. I was with a group I had yet to travel with, and on a canoe trip further north. Hurricane winds suddenly hit us while crossing a large lake. Rather than argue about what to do, we worked together as a team and quite easily survived one of the most dreadful storms I've ever seen.

Ever-changeable weather makes a camping life vivid and exciting. It's true that we look forward to clear skies. But it's also true that being tossed about in a violent windstorm or surviving a sudden cold spell brings a special element to the trip. It certainly can make it unforgettable.

Who would have thought it could still snow in May? York River, Ontario.

This is the moment you're glad you didn't go too cheap on your tent purchase.

KEEPING WARM AND DRY

I think it's a primitive instinct that comes out in all of us while camping — the desire to properly stormproof your camp. Just watch next time foul weather is brewing. Each member of your group of campers will try to share their two cents worth on how to prepare for the approaching weather front — especially men, and especially men with engineering degrees. I once went on a canoe trip with five engineers, the kind that design bridges for a living. The trip was going smoothly until a storm began to brew. One of the participants thought up some mathematical formula proving his theories on how to best stormproof the tents, and the others disagreed. All hell broke loose.

Being the writer of the group, I spent the time putting pen to paper and scribing all the points made throughout. They were all theories, of course. But none of the bridges the engineers built have yet to collapse, so these notes may be of some value.

First point made was to tie two 3-foot lengths of parachute cord at the front and back of the tent, attached to the poles and not the fabric, and to double stake each one. Second was positioning the tent door away from the prevailing winds to reduce the chance of water seepage, which makes a lot of sense since the tent's weakest link is the door's zipper. The third point, one that I believe in religiously, was to place a plastic tarp inside on the tent

Strange…it didn't call for rain before we left. The gang of engineers make preparations for an all-day downpour in Algonquin Park.

floor, not outside. Having it outside will just help collect the water. When the water begins to soak through, and it eventually will, having the tarp inside guarantees a protective layer between your sleeping pad and the soggy tent floor. Nylon guy lines also loosen when wet. So the group suggested attaching shock cord loops to each one. This would guarantee they'd keep taut and absorb any stress placed on the tent fly when the gale force winds begin to howl.

Once all the extra precautions were made and the storm hit, the group passed the time by also pointing out what should have been done before the

The Perfect Tarp Set-up

This is the most common set-up, in which the tarp is arranged "lean-to" style. Two ends are placed up high, preferably attached to a rope strung between two trees, and the other two placed low to the ground, positioned so the tarp acts as a shield between you and the prevailing winds. Make sure it's snug or the tarp will flap around in the wind and irritate you to no end throughout the night. And consider attaching small bungee cords on each corner grommet to help keep the ropes tight.

trip. Generous amounts of seam sealer should have been squeezed on the tent's seams. Extra stake loops should have been sewn to the sides of the tent since most designs only come with three or four, which is definitely not enough to stop the fly from flapping in the wind.

Also, when packing up the tent, stuffing it into its storage bag rather than rolling it was believed by the majority of the group to be far less harsh on the fabric and would add the extra bonus of reducing the bulk in your pack. And of course, they agree that the moment you got home the tent should be pitched in the backyard to properly dry it out; the moment mold and mildew set in, your tent will never hold up against wind and rain again.

Tips on Photographing the Perfect Sunset

- Use a tripod. It not only guarantees a sharper photo during low light conditions but also makes you focus on particular images you want to shoot.

- Turn off the flash mode.

- Don't be set on taking a photo of the entire sky; focus or even zoom in on a section of sky that most interests you.

- Make sure to include an object in foreground to create a three-dimensional image and bring more interest to the shot.

- Set the camera on manual focus. If you don't, the camera will have the background crisp but the foreground blurred.

- Set the camera on manual exposure, then take a meter reading with the sun near but not in the shot. Now, using that setting, take some photos. This process will keep your photos from being too dark.

- Don't put your camera away right away. Some of the best sunset shots are taken after the sun has just sunk below the horizon.

Red sky at night...sailor's delight.

A WISE SAILOR ONCE SAID...

Being an accurate weather forecaster while on trip will certainly get you respect. The only danger, of course, is that when you happen to get it wrong, you'll lose the respect faster than you got it in the first place.

Be wary of popular adages. Not all of them hold true. Others, however, have survived the test of time and are based on long-term observation and scientific reasoning. The general rule to follow is that any weather lore that relates to the appearance of the sky, movement of the clouds, wind change, or the reaction of flora and fauna to air pressure or humidity has some credibility. Everything else is just plain nonsense.

"Red sky at night, sailors delight. Red sky in the morning, sailors take warning." This is probably the most common as well as the most accurate of all the ancient adages. It's also been around the longest. It was Aristotle's

More Words of Weather Wisdom

"When leaves show their undersides, be very sure that rain betides."
The tale of leaves flipping upside down, showing their light-colored bottoms flickering in the breeze, is based on actual biological fact. The air temperature and wind alters significantly before an approaching storm. So when leaves curl up, which is a direct reaction from the high level of humidity and a quick change in wind direction, rain is definitely not far away.

Under the same principle of dropping air pressure, the lower the leaves turn on the tree the more severe the storm will be, meaning that if only the top of the tree is affected there's less chance of the rainfall being severe.

"Rain before seven, fine before eleven."
Weather patterns change more in early morning and evening. They are also generally in motion, never stagnant. So this statement, even though it's less valid than most, has some legitimacy.

"When halo rings the moon or sun, rain's approaching on the run."
Sun halos, or sundogs, or rings around the moon are excellent indicators of upcoming precipitation. The halo is formed when light from the sun or moon refracts as it passes through ice crystals formed by high-level cirrus and cirrostratus clouds. The clouds themselves don't produce rain or snow, but often denote an approaching low front that usually brings poor weather. This is same reason that a jet airplane's trail persists for several hours. Rain could arrive within one day.

"If your muscles all ache and itch, the weather fair will make a switch."
Again, low pressure usually foretells bad weather. Studies have also shown that most people who suffer from muscle aches and pains can foretell the drop in pressure. Nobody really seems to know why, however.

Windbound again. Lake Nipigon, Ontario.

pupil, Theophrastus of Eresus, who coined the actual phrase. But the first record of the aphorism is in the Bible (Matthew 16:23). Christ said "When it is evening ye say, it will be fair weather for the sky is red. And in the morning, it will be foul weather today for the sky is red and lowering." Shakespeare wrote, "A red morn that ever yet betokened, wreck to the seaman, tempest to the field..."

What it all means, basically, is that dry dust particles are in the atmosphere and can be easily seen during sunset and sunrise. Most storms move from west to east. So, with the sun setting in the west, the red sky at night usually indicates dry weather because those dry dust particles are being pushed towards you. With the sun rising in the east, the red sky in the morning indicates that the dust particles are being pushed away by an approaching low pressure.

Keeping an eye on the wildlife is a good way to forecast the weather as well. After all, they don't rely on the weather channel and have had to learn the hard way to deal with the elements on a day-to-day basis.

Ten minutes later we found ourselves storm-bound for three full days. Pukaskwa National Park, Lake Superior.

Watch birds in flight. When a low pressure hits, insects tend to stay low to the ground and the birds feeding on them can be seen doing the same. Woodpeckers are known to laugh louder and owls screech more before rain because the drop in barometric pressure and the rise in humidity cause an uncomfortable swelling in their ear tissue.

Mosquitoes also go out on a biting frenzy just before rain and crickets chirp quicker when warmer weather is on the way. Spiders spin webs during the mornings of dry, hot days and spin short webs or none at all if poor weather is imminent; some have even been known to break apart their webs just before a storm hits. Bees and hornets seen taking casual flights indicate a warm day but if they hover around their hives then poor weather is on the way.

Bees and wasps are also thought to be more likely to sting before an approaching storm. And the same goes for us humans. Experts in mental health have made the claim that a drop in barometric pressure makes us more irritable, and when the forecast changes from fair to foul, so do our moods. We also suffer lethargy, dizziness, headaches and depression. Our moods are even more short-lived and our energy levels and even pain tolerances decrease. What's to blame are ions in the air that affect the manufacture of serotonin, which is a hormone connected to our sleep cycle, emotions and sexual stimulation.

How depressing. Not only are we crankier when it's raining out, we opt to have less sex! No wonder weathermen have been known to lie about the forecast.

LIGHTNING DOES STRIKE TWICE

The sight of a lighting strike to a kayaker in the middle of an expansive lake or a ridge climber standing on a high peak can represents two things: the most terrifying experience ever had or the ultimate adrenaline rush. If you tend toward the second, then remember that the high you'll get does come with a price. One of the more common ways to die when you are outdoors is to be struck by lightning while sitting in a boat with, oddly enough, a graphite fishing rod stored behind you (the graphite rod acts as a perfect lightning rod). More people die by lightning in a year than in hunting accidents. More get hit and survive but suffer lifelong disabilities. But boy, it still is darn cool to watch the sky light up when a major storm hits.

In my youth I used to love watching storms roll in toward the campsite. But I was naïve. Recently I've seen too many nasty ones hit way too quickly. My daughter is in a stage of fascination with approaching storms and I want to tell her not to be afraid. It's difficult to do that, though, because I'm shaking in my boots as the thunder roars. Past experience has taught me to be afraid, very afraid. The only thing that helps settle my fear is a little knowledge of the velocity of what's about to hit and knowing ways to avoid getting hurt.

In temperate latitudes, storms are more common during late spring and summer months. A trip in September might be best if you can swing it. If not, then never try to muscle your way through a storm. Hunker down and wait it out. The real nasty ones only last a few minutes anyway.

Some kayakers and canoeists claim that you can paddle safely on the water during a lightning storm as long as you keep close to the shoreline. A protective "umbrella" is formed at about a forty-five-degree angle from you and the treetops along the bank. This is just a theory, however, and I think I'd rather take my chances on shore. Just make sure you put yourself and your shelter far away from any mound of high rock or tall tree. Also, the deeper you go into the woods the more chances of the lightning hitting another object. Keep as low as possible but don't lie flat out. Sit on top of a pack or, if you happen to be in the tent when the storm hits, squat on top of

Counting Down the Moments

Count the number of seconds (one Mississippi . . . two Mississippi . . . three Mississippi . . .) between the flash of lightning and the thunder. Then divide by five. You then have the distance in miles. The reasoning behind this calculation is that sound travels approximately a fifth of a mile per second. For example, in 5 seconds the strike is one mile away (3 seconds per kilometer); 10 seconds, it is 2 miles away; at 25 seconds, it's 5 miles away; and so on.

your sleeping pad with both feet close together. Then open the fly and watch the show. After all, you might as well be entertained by the magnificence of what's going on before a bolt strikes you blind.

In the majority of cases, victims of lighting strikes were injured or killed right at their campsite. But most of them were not struck directly by a single bolt. They were struck by the accompanying ground charge while lying asleep in their tents. Lightning is formed as a negative charge, from the base of the storm cloud passing over, inducing a positive charge where a negative charge usually is. The positive charge is pulled up and lightning is produced where there's an arc. If you're anywhere near the path of the lightning discharge, you can get zapped.

To create a thunderstorm, two specific elements are needed. Warm, moist unstable air needs to exist where there's some type of upward push. Intense heat, for example, can push the air upward, or a mountain standing

Yikes! Midday storm clouds roll in after a heat wave.

in the way of an advancing air mass can do the same, and so can a cold front moving in.

Watching the clouds is the best way to tell if the ingredients for bad weather are gathering up above. Clouds are excellent weather forecasters. Low fronts include stratus, nimbostratus, and cumulonimbus. Stratus are gray clouds that have a uniform flat base and usually bring light rain. Nimbostratus are darker gray and usually bring much heavier rainfall. Those dark, almost black clouds, with flat bottoms and towering thunderheads (looking something like an upside-down anvil) are cumulonimbus. They are a clear indicator of an approaching thunderstorm.

The middle groupings of clouds include altocumulus and altostratus. The altocumulus are made up of a sheet of white or gray cloudlets, sometimes formed in rows. The altostratus, striated and uniform in shape, spread across the sky in a thin gray layer. Both clouds formations tell of inclement weather, but with the altostratus you have at least twelve hours before it begins to rain.

Cirrus, cirrocumulus, and cirrostratus clouds form in high altitudes and are the least trustworthy forecasters. Cirrus clouds are separate, scattered wisps and usually indicate fair weather unless they become bunched together, meaning rain may fall the next day. Cirrocumulus clouds form a thin rippled pattern in the sky. They may grow perpendicularly throughout the day, and if the vertical growth does not disperse, a quick shower may follow. And finally, cirrostratus cloud, forming a transparent veil that creates a halo around the sun, is a prime indicator of a warm front; if it leads an altostratus cloud formation, "refreshing" rain could come down in less than 24 hours.

WATCHING THE NIGHT SKY

Weather forecast for tonight: dark.
— George Carlin

As usual it was a hectic morning dropping my three-year-old daughter off at daycare and then trying to escape in enough time so as not be late for work yet again. "Just one more story," she said as I headed for the door. It was the pouting look she gave me, an expression that always wins. So, I read her one more story.

The story I chose happened to end with a depiction of a young boy standing out in a field at night, in his pajamas, looking up at a starlit sky. It meant little to me at the time but fascinated Kyla. She instantly asked about the image and wondered why the boy was standing out in a field at night in his PJs.

My reply to her was quick, basically because I was still fixed on getting to work on time. "It's so he can look up at the rest of the universe," I said.

"But why?" she asked.

I must admit, it was a good question; after all, she had never been out past her bedtime yet and definitely hadn't stood in the middle of a field to gawk up to the heavens, so why would the boy in the book do such a silly thing? But again, I was late for work and so my response was quick — "I'll take you out tonight to see for yourself."

Like all children, Kyla remembered what I had promised and when I picked her up from daycare she was packed and all ready for her night hike and stargazing adventure. And come nightfall I kept to my word and walked her out to the middle of a cow pasture, wearing our pajamas, and we both stood and looked up toward the stars.

What we saw that evening surpassed what I had witnessed in all my years of camping. We saw the green trail of a meteor, hints of the Milky Way, Scorpio, Big Dipper, Little Dipper, Cygnus the swan, Draco the mighty

The Big Dipper

Many stories are told about Ursa Major — the Big Dipper. Native tribes of North America saw the ladle of the Big Dipper not as a bear's tail, but as hunters with dogs chasing the bear in circles around the northern heavens. Some tribes even connected the leaves changing color in the fall with the bear being wounded by the hunters and dripping its blood from the sky on to the trees.

Another common tale is from Greek mythology, in which the constellation is Callisto, a paramour of Zeus. It is said that Callisto swore a vow of chastity when she became a favorite hunting partner of Artemis, goddess of hunting. But one afternoon, while she was resting under a tree, Zeus caught a glimpse of her and was entranced by her beauty. He changed into the form of Artemis and approached Callisto. When she reached out to embrace her friend, Zeus showed his true form and had his way with her.

Zeus returned to Olympus and left poor Callisto pregnant. She later gave birth to a son, Arcas. Eventually Hera, the wife of Zeus, found out about her husband being unfaithful and took revenge on Callisto by transforming her into a bear, now making the hunter the hunted.

Callisto supposedly wandered through the woods for years, until one day she met up with her son, Arcas. When she went to him, however, he mistook her for a real bear and went to spear her. Zeus quickly intervened by changing Arcas into the same form as his mother. He grabbed them both by the tail and hurled them into heaven, stretching out their tails in the process.

When Hera found out that Zeus had saved Callisto, she once again showed her rage by demanding Tethys and Oceanus, gods of the sea and Hera's foster parents, never to allow the Great Bear to bathe. And to this day poor Callisto has yet to set below the horizon into the waters of the northern hemisphere.

The Little Dipper

The Little Dipper, more commonly known as Ursa Minor (Little Bear), was always thought to be the most important because it contained Polaris — the last star on the Little Dipper's handle and the brightest star in the sky. The Arabs called it the Guiding One. The Chinese named it Tou Mu, for a goddess who saved shipwrecked sailors with her supernatural powers and was later transported up into the sky. Ancient Norsemen called it the Hill of Heaven, home of the guardian of the rainbow bridge joining heaven and earth. Native North Americans believed it to be a young girl who appeared to a group of lost braves and showed them the way home. And according to Greek mythology (and the story of Callisto), the Little Bear is obviously Arcas, the Big Bear's son.

Enjoying the "silence" of a night sky — absolute bliss. Matagamasi Lake, Temagami.

Shooting Stars

- Meteor is the astronomical name given to a falling star and refers to the moment when a flash of light appears in the sky when a meteoroid or meteorite burns up as it enters the atmosphere.

- A meteoroid totally vaporizes when it enters the atmosphere but meteorites may not, allowing chunks of space rock to come crashing down to the earth's surface approximately 5,800 times per year.

- Bad Company, Poison, Harry Chapin and Bob Dylan all wrote hit songs titled "Shooting Star."

- Wishing upon a shooting star began in England in the Middle Ages, when it was believed the meteors were souls sent from heaven to announce a new birth.

- Islamic folklore says that a meteor was a missile-type weapon "launched" at evil-doers trying to sneak through the gates of heaven.

- "Shooting Star" was a character for Marvel Comics who first appeared in 1981. She was a Texan equipped with jet-boots and a six-shooter that shot star-shaped paralysis pellets.

dragon and quite possibly a UFO. She absolutely loved the event and went on about it endlessly at daycare the next morning, so much so I was late for work again. It was definitely worth it, though.

Kyla and I did what we humans have done for centuries. Astrology has been around for a long time and has played a major role in many cultures. Its origins were first thought to belong to the Greeks, and later the Egyptians. Some experts now claim it was initiated in the Americas. Inscriptions found at Metsamor and in the Geghama Mountain Range depict a stylish understanding of the universe before the Egyptians and even the Babylonians were watching and recording the heavens.

Also noteworthy is not when or who started looking up into the starlit evening sky but rather why. Navigation is a good guess. And so is spiritual worship. The Sumerians, who settled in Mesopotamia around 4000 BC, were thought to be the first group of people who worshipped the moon, sun and Venus, believing them to be gods, or the residence of gods.

The earliest cultures that studied the night sky did it in wilderness areas. And maybe the reason for that, beyond the fact that you can see more stars in remote areas away from unnatural light sources, is that gazing into the night sky does the same thing when you look upon vast wilderness — it humbles you. The immeasurable complexity of it all reminds you that we are mere specks here on earth; and like the stars themselves, we are born, grow old and turn into vapor. Looking up at the stars while on a camping trip goes beyond aesthetics. It's science based and philosophical; and, according to my daughter, it's a good darn reason to stand out in the middle of a field with your pajamas on.

MOON MAGIC

We all gaze up at it. We all admire it more when it's enlarged to its full potential. And we all wonder if Armstrong found any cheese on it during his 1966 visit. It can be a very uplifting experience to hike, kayak or canoe during a full moon. I've done it a few times and remember each time as if it were a dream. But how much do we really know about the moon?

For starters, it's the second-brightest object in the sky, meaning if you're floating around the universe with Captain Kirk and his crew you'd notice the moon before the planet earth. The moon also affects tides, as well as our moods. It's known to create "lunacy" and change people into werewolves. An ancient Jewish legend says that if one doesn't see their shadow in the moonlight, they are destined to die before the year is up. The term "harvest moon" comes from a bright moon lighting up the farm fields to allow for a longer working day during harvest time (and is the title of one of Neil Young's biggest albums). And we all know that when the moon hits your eye like a big pizza pie, you're in love.

There are times when not being able to find enough wood for a campfire can be a blessing in disguise. Chiniguichi Lake, Temagami.

But do you believe that the sun sets and the moon rises? The truth is, it doesn't work that way. The moon fully rotates around the earth in 27 days but it takes 29 days for a full moon to change over to another full moon. It may sound confusing, but the mixup in days is based on the fact that the earth is also orbiting the sun and the sun has everything to do with the fullness of the moon. This means the sun is never in the same place it was 27 days before. The moon also moves eastward and the earth has to move a little more to the east than the moon does so we can see it. Of course, that also means each moon "rise" is approximately 50 minutes later each evening.

The only time this is different is during September and October (harvest time) in the northern hemisphere (March and April in the southern hemisphere). At this time the moon takes a sharp turn north because the earth also changes its position. What this means (that we can see) is that a full moon in the fall comes up shortly after it the sun sets, giving a farmer extra time on the fields and a legendary musician a title for his song. A harvest moon appears bigger and brighter with a more golden or even reddish tone than most full moons. This is false, however. What you're seeing is an illusion. The gold or red color is actually the atmospheric haze you're looking

Many Moons Ago

The harvest moon is also called the singing moon or blood moon. A blue moon is the third full moon in a season that has four full moons. Mythology and folklore have given various names to each month's moon:

January – Wolf Moon	July – Hay Moon
February – Ice Moon	August – Corn Moon
March – Storm Moon	September – Harvest Moon
April – Growing Moon	October – Hunter's Moon
May – Hare Moon	November – Snow Moon
June – Mead Moon	December – Winter Moon

So, did Armstrong find any cheese up there?

Improving Your Night Vision

- Avoid any bright light up to an hour before heading out for a walk in the dark. Rod cells need at least 30 minutes to readjust, even after a brief burst of light.
- Use red light on your flashlight. Rod cells aren't affected by red light.
- Keep moving your head back and forth. Looking this way and that will trigger your peripheral vision.

- Avoid staring at one spot. This helps keep your rod cells from soaking in any light.
- It's true about eating carrots to improve night vision. Vitamin A allows for retinal, a chemical needed for your rods to function properly in low-light conditions. If you don't like carrots, try fortified milk and cheese and any dark leafy green veggies.

through while viewing the moon and is caused by the moon being lower in the horizon than normal. In fact, even stars look reddish in color when you spot them lower in the horizon. And the enlarged size is due to the horizon acting as a prism more than a lens, and even squishing the moon a fair bit as well. To prove this, simply stand on your head and look at the moon through your legs. The moon will be smaller because it is viewed on a higher angle then when standing upright. In performing this experiment, however, you may also be testing the "lunacy" theory; but who are we to judge?

NORTHERN LIGHTS

Northern lights are a dramatic display of red, green or even a mixture of the two lights, seemingly dancing across the night sky. They're known to only appear in the northern horizon or "polar zone." They are also known as aurora borealis, Aurora being the Roman goddess of dawn and borealis coming from the Greek for north wind. Its counterpart in the southern hemisphere is aurora australis, Australis being the Latin for of the south.

Like all other heavenly phenomena, the northern lights are linked to their fair share of myths and folklore. In Inuit legends the lights are spirits; and each region had different stories, from slain enemies trying to rise up to seek revenge to dancing children who died at birth. Other Native groups to the south believed the lights were from giant fires made from dwarfs who had caught whales with their bare hands and were boiling down the fat. Groups to the southeast believed them to be rival tribes boiling their enemies in giant pots. Others in the southwest thought the lights were the torches of giants spearing fish at night. Scandinavian culture saw the northern lights as dead virgins dancing in the sky. Skywatchers in China once believed the lights predicted the forthcoming birth of royalty. The oldest description written down was in the sixth century BC by Ezekiel, a prophet of ancient Israel: "A whirlwind came out of the north, a great cloud, and a fire infolding itself, and a brightness was about it, and out of the midst thereof as the color of amber, out of the midst of the fire."

The first to offer a real scientific explanation for the northern lights were Swedish astronomers Olof Hiorter and Anders Celsius back in 1741. They claimed that large magnetic fluctuations always happened when the northern lights were seen. They were headed in the right direction. Aurora borealis are created by solar winds, a stream of plasma coming from the sun, colliding with the edge of the earth's magnetic field. It's basically an electronic orgy of electrons, protons and atoms of gas with the higher energy emissions being shown in red colors and the lower levels in green. A mixture of the two gives one incredible light show.

To me, this is really confusing stuff and the complexity of it reminds me of Mark Twain's comment on trying to explain a rainbow. "We have not the reverent feeling for the rainbow that a savage has, because we know how it is made. We have lost as much as we gained by prying into that matter." Maybe northern lights, or any heavenly phenomena for that matter, are wilderness pleasures that don't need to be explained but just enjoyed. The next time you look up into the night sky and see the northern hemisphere lit up with dancing lights, don't worry if you don't understand it. Just watch and revel in it.

Tips on Photographing the Aurora

- The first point seems obvious but should be stated — turn off the flash mode.

- Place camera on sturdy tripod.

- Set the camera to manual exposure or shutter priority.

- Experiment with different time settings for the shutter to be open — starting around thirty seconds and going as long as the camera will stay open (i.e., five or even ten minutes).

- For even longer exposures, you need to set the camera on "bulb," which means the camera shutter will be open until you decide it to be closed. Refer to your camera's manual for this one; some models actually have "bulb" or "B" on the exposure setting and for some you need a remote for the camera that's usually sold separately.

- Pushing the button on the camera with your finger may cause some blurriness; use the remote or set the timer.

- You could also experiment with cranking up the ISO or ASA setting, which determines how sensitive the camera is to light. If you're using a film, not digital camera, then you can purchase higher ISO or ASA film speeds from 400 to 800. Some digital cameras can be set as high as 1600. Take note, however, that the higher the number the grainier the film and less resolution a digital image will have.

St. Elmo's Fire

When the space between the ground and the clouds is electrically charged during a thunderstorm, a "glow discharge" called St. Elmo's Fire is created. The electricity created is drawn to the closest and highest conductor — for instance, something like a church steeple or ship's mast. The name was actually derived from St. Erasmus, the patron saint of sailors. The seamen believed the blue glow on top of the yardarms was the saint protecting them from the onslaught of the storm.

SOMEWHERE OVER THE RAINBOW

Somewhere over the rainbow, skies are blue, and the dreams that you dare to dream really do come true.
— E.Y. Harburg, "Over the Rainbow"

Maybe it's because I'm of Irish descent, but I really like rainbows. I'm not alone. Rainbows have been used since the beginning of civilization to symbolize good things. And maybe I'm just a dreamer, but I believe that spotting something that historically has been used to represent optimism has to create a positive experience on any camping trip.

In Greek mythology, rainbows were the path used by the Iris, messenger for the gods, to travel between heaven and earth. The Norse believed the rainbow was the bridge connecting the dwelling place of humans and gods. In Chinese mythology, the rainbow is a slit in the sky that was plugged up with stones of five different colors by Goddess Numa. Christianity and Judaism used it to symbolize God's promise that no more floods would come. The Irish leprechaun hid his pot of gold at the end of the rainbow. In the 16th century, the rainbow flag flew for the first time to symbolize hope and social change to peasants; today it is seen on the flag during San Francisco's gay pride parade. Greenpeace's mother ship *Rainbow Warrior* was named after the Cree prophecy "When the world is sick and dying, the people will rise up like warriors of the rainbow." Woolf's great literature uses it to highlight man's mortality: "It was all as ephemeral as a rainbow." Judy Garland sang "Over the Rainbow" in the movie *The Wizard of Oz* to show a young girl's desire to escape the troubles of the modern world, from "the sadness of raindrops" to a better world "over the rainbow."

It's believed that sometime during the late 1200s a Persian astronomer, Qutb al-Din al-Shirazi, gave the first real and accurate explanation for the rainbow. A few years later Robert Grosseteste, and then shortly after, Roger Bacon, experimented with light being directed through a crystal and then water droplets displaying the colors of the rainbow. However, it was Rene

Over the Rainbow

Hundred of famous musicians have recorded their own version of "Over the Rainbow," first sung by Judy Garland, including:

Alice Cooper	Eric Clapton	Mariah Carey
Aretha Franklin	The Flaming Lips	Metallica
Barbra Streisand	Frank Sinatra	Queen
Bette Midler	Jerry Lee Lewis	The Ramones
Bob Marley	Jimi Hendrix	Ray Charles
Carly Simon	Kenny G	Tiny Tim
Dave Bowie	Harry Connick Jr.	Tom Jones
Deep Purple	Phil Collins	Uncle Cracker
Doris Day	Placido Domingo	
Erasure	The Platters	

Descartes in 1637 who gave a logical explanation of the "bow" phenomena and, not long after, Isaac Newton who figured out the color spectrum.

The moment you spot a rainbow is when there are water droplets in the air and sunlight is striking from behind you. You also must be low to the ground or at least at a low angle. The best results come when half the sky is still darkened by the rain clouds and the other half is lit up by the approaching sun, and you're looking at the dark sky ahead of you with the sun shining from behind you. These moments are rare, of course, and more uncommon than you would think. In climates where rainbows are more usually formed, you'd be lucky to spot more than ten in one year. Anywhere else, if you see three, consider yourself blessed.

Rainbows are optical and meteorological phenomena. They are an optical illusion, which is why the leprechaun's pot of gold can never be found. A spectrum of light arcs across the sky when sunlight penetrates droplets of moisture. As it enters the water, the light is first refracted, then reflected off the back of the raindrop, and once again refracted. The "bow" or arc of the rainbow is centered on the shadow of the observer's head. Because the light hits at various angles, the colors vary. The color red appears on the outside and violet on the inside. On rare occasions a secondary rainbow is seen outside the primary arc and with opposite color schemes, meaning violet on the outside and red on the inside. The colors in between the primary and secondary (outside and inside) colors vary but the sequence listed by Isaac Newton was red, orange, yellow, green, blue, indigo and violet.

Rainbows apologize for angry skies.

— Sylvia Voirol

Looking for the pot of gold at the end of the rainbow. St. Nora Lake, Haliburton, Ontario.

More Neat Facts About Rainbows

- Rainbows are rarely seen in the winter because the two key elements are rain and sunshine. Water droplets usually freeze into ice particles that don't create rainbows.

- Rainbows are rare during midday because the center of the rainbow's circle is always opposite the sun and the observer has to be at the same level to be able to see the phenomena itself.

- No person sees the same rainbow. Each rainbow is owned by a single viewer. This is because the distribution of colors is never at the same angle for each viewer and are therefore different for each viewer.

- If the rainbow is close so is the storm, and if it is far away, the storm is also a good distance away.

10

EXPLORATION
The Joys of Living to Tell the Tale

*An adventure is never an adventure while it's happening.
Challenging experiences need time to ferment, and adventure
is simply physical and emotional discomfort recollected
in tranquillity.*

— Tim Cahill

WHEN YOU THINK ABOUT IT, THE MODERN-DAY IDEA OF traveling in the outdoors didn't really exist a century ago. People didn't go camping to enjoy themselves — they had a more direct and functional purpose. Mountain climbers took on a summit for measurements, hikers wandered the wilderness to shoot game or find gold, and canoeists flushed down rapids to discover a new trade route. It wasn't until the beginning of the 20th century that people started going outdoors for fun more than employment. And before that, having a misadventure was something you would avoid at all costs. But nowadays it almost as if it's something you're secretly hoping for.

Look at canoe tripping, for example. It's said that canoe tripping in a wilderness area is an absorbing, emotional and life-altering experience. It's a time of beauty, elegance and simplicity. It's even believed by some to offer a moment of spiritual awakening. But if that's the case, then why do I always find myself spinning tales of mishap out there? My writing has always highlighted the horrible experiences over the trips that went really well. But isn't that the way it is for everyone? If you spend the day pushing a flimsy canoe across choppy water, carry your gear across mud-filled portages, sleep on the hard ground inside a tent the size of a doghouse, and suffer greatly from

If you're too exhausted to carry the canoe any further, then dragging it behind you will suffice, as long as it's not your canoe, of course. The author looks for water in Temagami.

biting black flies, mosquitoes, horseflies and pesky no-see-ums, don't you want to tell somebody about it? Occasionally I wonder just how many non-paddlers are put off paddling after reading my thoughts about how nasty it is.

Here's the catch. It's a given to all canoeists that the splendor of wilderness canoeing is the good that always outweighs the bad. But if you ask any paddler to reminisce about their favorite wilderness trip it will always be their most difficult, grueling, nightmarish misadventure. Why is that? Why do they yearn to return long after the mishap has occurred? Why does the pain they once suffered become a fading memory? And more important, why do they enjoy wilderness canoe tripping even more after the punishment of wicked portages and hordes of bugs?

Surely the basis of a meaningful answer has to be more than how a marathon runner would explain why they do what they do. It has to be more substantial than a simple physical enjoyment or a buzz of endorphins. And it definitely has to be more powerful than answering a beckoning curiosity of what's out there.

I've come to the conclusion, after having countless good and bad times while canoe tripping in remote areas of the north, that it is the real but often exaggerated dangers that help highlight your kinship with wilderness itself. The challenges of wilderness stimulate us all, so much so for some of us that it doesn't count as a wilderness trip without some kind of hardship or misadventure.

"Anyone pack the saw?" Our group looks for the portage along northwestern Ontario's Kopka River.

KNOWING WORSE TRIPS THAN YOURS

I tend to read only books that deal with canoeing mishaps. It's a tad embarrassing. My wife, who belongs to a book club and reads a book a week, covering everything from religious philosophy to cheap romance, is always on my case telling me to open my horizons. She says I should at least try to look beyond canoe literature. So, to appease her I went off to the small local bookstore a few months back to pick up a Harry Potter novel, only to come back with the movie from the neighborhood video store.

So why is it that I indulge only in books on bad canoe trips? What weird gratification do I get out of reading how things went wrong for someone else? I think maybe it's because hearing someone else's tales of misery makes my own bad trips seem not so bad. Here are a few of my favorites:

Women Know Best

This one's a classic. It starts off in 1903 with two writers from New York, Leonidas Hubbard and Dillon Wallace, and a Native guide, George Elson, setting out to explore an uncharted river in northern Labrador. Near the start they take a wrong turn, ending up on the wrong river, and poor Hubbard ends up dying of starvation. The other two walk out and Wallace returns to New York to write a book about the ill-fated voyage. Mina, Hubbard's widow, is infuriated with how Wallace characterizes her husband in the book and when he decides to head out again to paddle the proper river this time, Mina plans her own trip to Labrador, hoping to beat Wallace to the chase. In the end, Wallace gets lost again and Mina, guided by George Elson, wins the race — and is believed to have a secret love affair with George along the way.

The Amazon or Bust

Don Starkell's 20,000-kilometer canoe trip, from Winnipeg to the mouth of the Amazon River, is one heck of an amazing canoe trip. Starkell set out on his 23-month journey accompanied by his two sons, Dana and Jeff, in 1980. The first year they endured numerous capsizes and lost precious supplies to the rough seas out on the Gulf. That's when the one son, Jeff, called it quits and left the expedition, believing his father and brother were absolutely insane to continue. Don and Dana headed out again the next spring, however, and before winter they found themselves being shot at, robbed, arrested, jailed and very close to being executed by a pair of inebriated gunmen. The third and final season the pair traveled up the Orinoco River and then down the Rio Negro to the Amazon River and eventually to its mouth at Belem, Brazil. But not before almost starving to death, getting severe food poisoning, and completing a 45-mile portage along a cart track through a mosquito-infested jungle. *The Guinness Book of World Records* registered it as the longest canoe trip ever. Critics called it an amazing account of courage and commitment. Some common canoeists think it was just a crazy trip done by a couple of naive paddlers who were darn lucky to survive. Anyway you look at it though, it still deserves to be mentioned as a classic canoe misadventure.

In Search of the North West Passage

The only thing George Back ever did wrong during his three Arctic expeditions in the early 1800s is that he traveled with Sir John Franklin. By sheer luck, George Back survived Franklin's endless series of mishaps (Franklin didn't). They were in search of the mythical North West Passage and along the way they dealt with starvation, cannibalism, mutiny and murder. As payment, Back was allowed to name a river after himself, but not until he nearly drowned more than once during the descent and almost froze to death while dragging his boat back upstream before winter closed in. When he returned for his last exploration of Arctic he kept clear of canoeing rivers in the Barren Lands and chose to sail across Hudson Bay instead. His ship ended up drifting in pack ice for over ten months and the crew suffered miserably from scurvy. Luckily for him, he reconsidered returning with Franklin on his final and fatal expedition, and decided to stay home.

No Glory for the Poor Working Stiff

It seems that most of the canoe misadventures you hear about are of great explorers heading out in some less-than-modest attempt to conquer nature. Along the way they either perish or come uncomfortably close to expiring, and then become famous for it. But what about the poor working stiff who just happens to get into a jam while being employed in the north? For example, the only reason R. King Pettigrew went out into the nowhere-land of the Northwest Territories back in 1939 was to work as a surveyor and collect the $60 a month salary from the Geological Survey of Canada. Who knew that along the way he and his guide, Joe Robertson, would manage to dump in some frothy rapids only two weeks into their trip, losing everything they had except for a butcher knife. The knife was used to repair the canoe, hunt down caribou, and then make clothing out of the caribou hide. Not only did they survive, they finished their survey job and got paid — minus deductions for the lost gear, of course.

Group Dynamics 101

Finding out you dislike your canoe partner on a trip can be a bit of a bother, especially if it's a two-year trip beginning at the foot of 42nd Street in New York and ending in Nome, Alaska. Jeff Pope and Shell Taylor's aversion for one another began just a few days into their epic voyage of 1936. But they managed to hold off punching one another; at least until the second-last day. The two went fists to cuffs, beating each other to a pulp, and then called the match a draw before going home, never to tell the story in print until 50 years later.

Windbound on Lake Winnipeg

It can be the simplest of things that can endanger one's life out on a canoe trip. For example, during Alec Ross's 5,000-kilometer trip from Ottawa to Vancouver his worst misfortune is when a sudden wind takes his beloved canoe down the beach and severely damages it while he's windbound on Lake Winnipeg. At first, this doesn't sound so bad. But anyone who's witnessed the wrath of Lake Winnipeg would know that this remote setting is definitely not a good place to be marooned. Like any true explorer, though, he didn't let his misfortune get him down. In fact, he even "perversely" enjoyed the challenge — and luck prevailed. Ross found an old toolbox along the beach, which oddly enough contained just the right equipment to fix the broken boat.

Thank goodness it was a rental canoe. Mishap along the Mississagi River, Kawarthas.

Top 49 Misadventure Reads

1. Historical journals of Samuel de Champlain (1567–1635)

2. *Alexander Mackenzie's Voyage to the Pacific Ocean*, Alexander Mackenzie (1793)

3. David Thompson journals (1804–1805)

4. Lewis and Clark journals (1804)

5. Simon Fraser journals (1808)

6. *By Canoe Down the Coppermine*, John Richardson, with the Franklin expedition (1821)

7. *Peace River: A Canoe Voyage from Hudson's Bay to Pacific*, Sir George Simpson (1828)

8. *A Thousand Miles in the Rob Roy Canoe on Rivers and Lakes of Europe*, J. MacGregor (1866)

9. *Canoeing in the Dismal Swamp*, John Boyle O'Reilly (1890)

10. *Voyage of the Paper Canoe: A Geographical Journey of 2500 Miles from Quebec to the Gulf of Mexico*, Nathaniel H. Bishop (1874)

11. *The Canoe Aurora: A Cruise from the Adirondacks to the Gulf*, Dr. Chas. A. Neide (1885)

12. *A Week on the Concord and Merrimack Rivers*, Henry David Thoreau (1849)

13. *Hubbard–Wallace Labrador Expedition*, Wallace (1903)

14. *The Tent Dwellers*, Albert Bigelow Paine (1908)

15. *The Arctic Prairies: A Canoe Journey of 2,000 Miles in Search of the Caribou*, Ernest Thompson Seton (1911)

16. *Lands Forlorn: A Story of an Expedition to Hearn's Coppermine River*, George M. Douglas (1914)

17. *Dangerous River*, R.M. Patterson (1920)

18. *The Survival of the Bark Canoe*, John McPhee (1931)

19. *True North*, Elliot Merrick (1933)

20. *Canoeing with the Cree: A 2,250-mile Voyage from Minneapolis to Hudson Bay*, Eric Sevareid (1935)

21. *Tales From an Empty Cabin*, Grey Owl (1938)

22. *The Incomplete Angler*, John D. Robins (1943)

23. *Sleeping Island*, P.G. Downes (1943)

24. *Nahanni Trailhead*, Joanne Ronan Moore (1952)

25. *Goodbye to a River*, John Grave (1960)

26. *The Singing Wilderness*, Sigurd Olson (1956)

27. *Canoeing with the Cree*, Eric Sevareid (1968)

28. *Down the River North*, Constance Helmericks (1968)

29. *Deliverance*, James Dickey (1970)

30. *The Last Wilderness*, Peter Browning (1975)

31. *The Complete Wilderness Paddler*, James West Davidson and John Rugge (1976)

32. *Ultimate North: Canoeing Mackenzie's Great River*, Robert Douglas Mead (1976)

33. *Paddle to the Amazon*, Don Starkell (1980)

34. *Cold Summer Wind*, Clayton Klein (1983)

35. *New York to Nome: The True Story of Two Men and the Adventure of a Lifetime (a 1936 expedition)*, Rick Steber (1987)

36. *Freshwater Saga*, Eric W. Morse (1987)

37. *One Incredible Journey*, Verlen Kruger (1987)

38. *Path of the Paddle*, Bill Mason (1988)

39. *Where Rivers Run*, Gary and Joanie McGuffin (1988)

40. *In the North of Our Lives: A Year in the Wilderness of Northern Canada*, Christopher Norment (1989)

41. *Water and Sky*, Allan Kesselheim (1989)

42. *Magnetic North: A Trek Across Canada*, David Halsey (1990)

43. *Distant Fires*, Scott Anderson (1990)

44. *Summer North of Sixty: By Paddle and Portage Across the Barren Lands*, James Raffan (1990)

45. *Into the Great Solitude*, Robert Perkins (1991)

46. *Coke Stop in Emo: Adventures of a Long-Distance Paddler*, Alec Ross (1995)

47. *A Death on the Barrens*, George James Grinnell (1996)

48. *The Hummingbird From Resolute: Memories of a Journey to the Polar Sea*, David C. Whyte (1997)

49. *Canoeing a Continent: On the Trail of Alexander Mackenzie*, Max Finkelstein (2002)

James Dickey's *Deliverance* is probably not the best book to pack along on your first canoe trip.

Post-Trip Blues

David Halsey's 1977 wilderness trek across Canada went from bad to worse. First his crew quit four days into the trip — taking most of the gear and leaving Halsey ill-equipped and alone. He continued on, however, and was later joined by a young photographer (Peter Souchuk) and Ki, a scruffy half-wild dog, who ventured into camp one evening begging for food and never left. The threesome managed to survive canoe spills and severe frost-bite before they reached their destination (a small town along the St. Lawrence River, Quebec) three years later. But it was when Halsey returned home that things really got tough. The 23-year-old had severe problems dealing with the "real world" and began treatments for manic depression. His problem worsened when his dog, Ki, was struck by a car. It wasn't long before the explorer took an overdose of medication and drove off a bridge, dying in hospital shortly after. This is one tale about a young man's passion to live in the wilderness and his bitter attempt to return to modern society.

The 20th Century Comes Crashing Down

The whole point, when Christopher Norment and his five buddies headed out for a two-year canoe trip from Canada's Yukon to Hudson Bay, was to leave the technology of the modern world behind. That's why it's so ironic that the wreckage of the Cosmos 954 nuclear satellite chose to smack into the earth only a few kilometers away from their winter camp at Warden's Grove. The tone of the trip changes dramatically when the crews' peaceful solitude is disturbed by serious military types, dressed in full radiation suits, who invade their camp and immediately take them away for "testing." There's no other canoe "misadventure" that can compare to this one.

Slogging up the Rat River

Verlen Kruger didn't start paddling until he was 41. But he sure made up for his late start. This proclaimed "paddling messiah" has clocked over 100,000 miles (equivalent to three-and-and-half times around the world). Along the way he's had more "misadventures" than all of the rest of us combined. But his slog up the Rat River, a route that gains more than 1,200 vertical feet in less than 40 miles, has to be one of his most nightmarish moments spent in a canoe. It was just a short section of his 7,000-mile trip from Montreal to the Baring Sea, which he happened to complete in only one season, but en route Kruger and his partner, Clinton Waddell, faced flooded waters, freezing temperatures, continuous rainfall, snow flurries, soaking-wet gear, and even a few wrong turns. Kruger claimed it was God, and Waddell's "fortified pancakes," that got them through it all. However they did it, it was one phenomenal adventure that no doubt would change a person's life forever.

To Catch a Moose

In 1908 Albert Bigelow Paine and his trusty sidekick, Eddie, paddled, bush-whacked and mucked their way through the wilderness of Nova Scotia on a mission of grave scientific importance. Their objective: to catch two moose calves to stick in the British Museum. Along the way they dealt with a very leaky tent, an upset stomach from eating an owl, an argument over corrupt reading material (Paine brought "Alice in Wonderland" and Eddie packed along a French sex novel), and a severe bout of poison ivy. They failed in catching a moose, dead or alive, and went back home to New York the moment they ran low on their medical supply for treating poison ivy — whisky.

RIVER PADDLING

"It's little Anxious," he said to himself, "to be a Very Small Animal Entirely Surrounded by Water. Christopher Robin and Pooh could escape by Climbing Trees, and Kanga could escape by Jumping, and Rabbit could escape by Burrowing, and Owl could escape by Flying, and Eeyore could escape by — by making a Loud Noise Until Rescued, and here am I, surrounded by water and I can't do anything."
— Piglet, in *Winnie-the-Pooh*, by A.A. Milne

I look like a geek dressed up as a playboater, but now and then I'm per-suaded by my peers to slip into an embarrassingly tight wetsuit, neoprene booties and a helmet the color of Neapolitan ice cream and then join them in attempting Stern Squirts, High Rock Boofs, Pirouettes, McTwists, Hairy Ferries and the ultimate Mystery Move — the conversion of a canoe into a submarine, sometimes intentional and sometimes not. Of course, I've yet to master any of these moves. Sometimes I wonder if it's just the greasy ham-burgers we order at the local pub after the event is done that really attracts me to the sport.

What I much prefer is not playboating for the day but river tripping. Messing around rapids is definitely addictive, but not as much as being pulled down current on a remote wilderness river for a week or two. It's a great feeling a canoeist gets the moment your boat is at the brink of some run or being tossed around a thick wall of water, and suddenly realize there's no turning back — you are now at the mercy of the river gods. But beyond the rush it gives, moving water also bestows upon you an unsur-passed, three-dimensional view of the natural world that engulfs the water-way itself. River tripping is about celebrating water and the landscape

"I think we could have run that." Len Lockwood on the Petawawa River.

around it. When you run the length of a watershed you learn the full character of the river and more deeply understand the importance of each part of the watershed. You also get to know its importance to the ecosystem.

River running also makes you feel like a kid again. As a child, I spent days floating down the local creek on a slab of white foam or just sitting on the banks watching a flume of water dance over the rocks. I was entranced by it all and believed what writer, Roderick L. Haig-Brown, believed — "I have never yet seen a river that I could not love." The magic of moving water is all throughout great literature. A.A. Milne's Winnie-the-Pooh rejoiced in the art of playing "Pooh-sticks." Twain's Huckleberry Finn felt it and marveled at the breadth of the Mississippi. Thoreau discussed it in *A Week on the Concord and Merrimack Rivers*. Later it was Edward Abbey and John McPhee. Loren Eisley claimed in her book *The Immense Journey* that "If there is magic on this planet, it is contained in water."

Running a river is a thrilling experience not to be missed. It has an exciting beginning, a definite end (sometimes tragic), points of interest along the way, a trip full of ups and downs, and on the most challenging drops there's always an easy way out — something called the portage.

LOVING TO PORTAGE

It's not that I enjoy the idea of carrying a heavily loaded pack through boot-sucking muck, falling backwards on the trail and ending up like an upturned turtle, or watch helplessly while blood-thirsty mosquitoes suck blood out of my knuckles. But I think the art of portaging does have some worthwhile benefits. Let's start with the simple pleasures. It gives you a time out, a moment to relieve yourself of that nasty canoe butt, an itchy rash you get on your toosh after sitting in a sodden canoe seat all day. Each take-out also acts as a pee break area, which is probably why it's wise never to harvest blueberries from bushes neighboring the beginning of a portage trail. It's

"Take the darn picture Kevin, this canoe is getting heavy!" Andy Baxter, Mississagi River, Kawarthas.

Eight Ways to Relieve the Pain of Portaging

- Splurge on either renting or buying a lightweight canoe. It's worth it.

- Strap your extra gear, such as paddle and fishing rods along the inside gunwale of the canoe with bungee cords.

- Do yourself a big favor and buy a good customized yoke and place it on the canoe yourself. Most canoes come with cheap models and are placed dead center. I like mine set slightly back from center, making the canoe a little tail heavy.

- Before you set the canoe down for a break, try to go a little further by altering your grip; hold the left gunwale, the right, then both, then go from holding the gunwales to grasping a carrying bar placed directly in front of you or the end of a rope tied to the bow.

- Pace yourself. Walk twenty minutes, which equals 2,000 yards (approximately 1000 meters) and then rest, treat yourself to a gummy bear or hard candy and continue on.

- Sing a song (a good song) to pass the time or daydream of past (or present) girlfriends or boyfriends.

- A tump strap can help spread the stress of the load and stops the canoe from slipping down your back. Take note, however, that a tump may not be for everyone because it tests the neck muscles.

- Be fair in sharing the load with trip members, and stay organized at the take-out and put-in, assigning gear to each person to minimize lost equipment.

Ouch! Now that's gotta hurt.

The infamous Kopka Falls portage. Yes, it's a nasty one.

also a great place to spot wildlife, such as bull moose in full rut or a nuisance bear waiting patiently for unsuspecting canoeists to leave their food pack for the second trip across.

These are, however, only minimal delights. There's a far bigger reward for anyone who wishes to suffer the pain of a severe carry through the bush. What I love about a nasty portage is that the more it hurts, the more removed you become from the stress of the "civilized" world. I can pretty much guarantee that the portager who suffers the most will be enriched the most. A 2-kilometer portage, with a few steep inclines and maybe a bug-infested swamp or two in between, will give you complete wilderness solace. There are definitely no crowds at the end, and if you manage to come across another paddler, it's guaranteed they'll be just as insanely in love with the pain and pleasures of portaging as you are.

Canoeists generally have two different kinds of portage strategies; you either carry everything across in one trip or go back for a second load. The single carry is much more effective when you're in a hurry, not to mention it greatly reduces the amount of bug bites you'd get along the trail. One person carries the hefty canoe along with an even heftier pack strapped to his or her back. The other is burdened with one monstrous pack, or worse, two medium-size packs, one on top of the other. But those who go back for a second load not only greatly reduce the weight of each carry, they can also add much more gear on to their luxury list, and at the same time add much more fun to the trip when it's time to call it a day. Privileges at camp include appetizing meals, washed down with an extra glass of wine, while seated in a cozy camp chair. Single carriers have to resort to freeze-dried spam, taken with a bland cup of herbal tea, while squatting on a clump of wet moss.

Pure happiness lies somewhere in between, however, It's called "the trip-and-a-half" method, and it's the best way to get yourself across any lengthy bug-ridden trail. Both paddlers head across the portage, one with a pack — and maybe a smaller pack resting on top — and the other the canoe. Halfway along the one carrying the canoe stops, puts his or her load down, and then returns for the second pack. The person carrying the first pack continues on to the end, and then returns for the canoe. If only one person in the group is able to carry the canoe, then just alter it so you both start off with packs, and one person goes back for the canoe. Either way, you are only walking the portage one-and-a-half times rather than three.

SHARING BEAR STORIES

If an animal does something, we call it instinct; if we do the same thing for the same reason, we call it intelligence.

— Will Cuppy

Of all the stories told after a trip, bear encounters have to be at the top of the list. In general, campers are terrified of bears; they always have been and most likely always will. Even if the statistics clearly show that you have a greater chance of being hit on the highway driving to your camping destination

Seconds after this photo was shot the bear took a number of swipes at the bow of my canoe before it moved on. Seriously, I have witnesses.

than being mauled to death, the bear encounter is still thought to be more problematic.

Personally, I've had some really bad luck dealing with bears. A bear biologist once suggested that it was due to my fear of the animal, explaining that if a bear senses any anxiety, he will use it to his advantage. His theory actually makes sense. I had a bear scare me off my campsite and then steal a chocolate cake I was in the middle of baking. I had a bear bully me away from my camp gear while on a portage and then steal a tube of toothpaste from my pack. I had a bear harass me the moment I pulled into a park visitor center parking lot and then attempt to steal, oddly enough, my Thermos of coffee. And I must admit that each time I was absolutely horrified.

I also have to admit, though, that there is a silver lining to surviving a bad bear encounter — you get to tell everyone the story.

My favorite bear tale happened at a campground in northern Ontario, situated on Missinaibi Lake. The bear had pestered me for two days, always sneaking in around the supper hour to steal an evening meal. On day three I couldn't stand it any longer. The moment he strolled into my site I threw a rock at him and hit him directly in the ass. What a bad move.

In retrospect, camping at the campground was just a poor decision. A few weeks before I had stopped to camp here while paddling down the Missinaibi River and was confronted by the same darn bear. He walked through my site with someone's roasted chicken in his mouth. Now, after deciding to drive back here after my trip to relax for a few days, I found the bear still hanging around harassing campers, including me.

I'm not sure why I snapped and lost control. I was stressed, however, and had a sudden urge not to let the bear intimidate me any longer. I tried banging pots at first. That didn't seem to work. So I tossed a small boulder his way. He gave me a stare, as if to say "That was stupid," and then charged me. The bear ran full tilt toward me, stopping dead only a few feet away to beat the ground in front of him with his front paws, while snapping and

Death by...

Being killed by a bear is the least of your worries. Here are the top five ways people die in the wilderness according to the National Safety Council:

- Sitting in a boat and being hit by lightning because you have a graphite fishing rod stored in the boat.
- Drowning during boating activity.
- Hypothermia by submersion in cold water.
- Allergic reaction to wasps or bees.
- Cataclysmic storms.

growling. It was a classic fake charge (of course, I didn't know that at the time). I responded by waving my arms up in the air and yelling obscenities at him. And then, surprisingly, the bear ran away.

That's when I should have called it quits. But instead I took it further by chasing the bear out of my campsite. Maybe because I had terrible flashbacks of being bullied back in grade school, but I copied the bear's actions by beating the ground and making snapping and growling noises. The strategy worked. He left my site, but not before swatting the bow of my canoe with his paw a few times. It was the oddest thing. He ran straight past three aluminum boats and one kayak. Then he put the brakes on while passing my boat, gave it a sniff, started bashing it, and then sauntered off in a huff.

He definitely was a bear with an attitude.

WHAT WE REALLY FEAR IS...

Fear makes the wolf bigger than he is.

— German proverb

Last spring, on the way to speak at a local library on the joys of canoeing, I witnessed a terrible accident along the highway. Some young kid zipped past an older couple, who then slammed on the brakes, causing a chain reaction of smashed-up cars. I stopped to help out and began immediately administering first-aid to the older couple. The passenger had serious cuts to her face and arms from broken glass and her husband, the driver, was pinned behind the steering wheel. He later died in hospital.

When arriving at the library I gave, surprisingly, one of my best shows of the speaking tour. I've never been so enthusiastic about letting people know about the pleasures of wilderness canoe tripping. It was as if I was using memories of past canoe excursions to rid my thoughts of what had just happened on the way to the show. Then, just as I was wrapping up the talk, a woman in the back row put up her hand and asked a simple question "Isn't it dangerous out there?"

My answer was just as simple. "No, definitely not! The perception of a wilderness trip being dangerous may be real, but in fact it's our civilized world, like driving on a highway, that's truly dangerous."

On the way home that night I thought about a particular trip that made me even surer about my response to the question. It was a few years back, at the end a lengthy and very remote river trip. Our bush pilot, who was scheduled to pick us up that day, had been arrested for being involved in a pornography scandal…. I definitely didn't see that one coming.

Now our crew was stuck waiting patiently for another pickup, which we were told could be two or three more days. Our food supply for five con-

"Did you hear something? I thought I heard something...you sure you didn't hear something?" Ashley McBride battles bear phobia in Algoma.

sisted of half a bag of GORP, a package of instant potatoes, a dozen prunes, and, quite possibly, a tame rabbit who was naively hanging around our camp looking for companionship. We had limited battery supply for our satellite phone because one of our members insisted on calling his wife twice a day throughout the trip; another member was hung over; and we were informed by the air service that both the shuttle vehicles we had left waiting for us, parked at the end of an 80-kilometer dirt road, had been vandalized (flat tires) by some local activists who didn't like canoeists in their secret fishing grounds.

It had not been a good week. We were paddling upstream the entire trip, on a route that was more than a little confusing. Portages were overgrown and water levels were low enough that we left a trail of canoe paint on the river bed just as Hansel and Gretel left bread crumbs through the Black Forest. The only way out was to paddle six more days or wait for another plane to arrive, hopefully flown by a law-abiding Baptist minister with anti-porn beliefs.

After that incident, I came to the conclusion that I spend a little too much time worrying about marauding bears, violent storms or becoming lost. Sometimes, what you're trying to escape back home can still inflict itself upon you out there, and can actually be far more dangerous. Heck, I say, bring on the bears, the storms, and the not knowing where I am. I'd rather deal with the dangers of the wild than the evils of the civilized world.

11

INTRINSIC VALUES OF WILDERNESS

Ask the men who have known it and who have made it part of their lives. They might not be able to explain, but your very question will kindle a light in eyes that have reflected the camp fires of a continent, eyes that have known the glory of dawns and sunsets and nights under the stars. Wilderness to them is real and this they do know; when the pressure becomes more than they can stand, somewhere back of beyond, where roads and steel and towns are still forgotten, they will find release.

— Sigurd Olson, *American Forests*

FOR EIGHTEEN YEARS NOW I'VE TAUGHT AN ENVIRONMENTAL issues course on a part-time basis at a local college and I'm more puzzled about the subject now than I ever have been. I've spent all those years lecturing on the severity of our problems and our different attitudes to fixing them. The trouble, of course, is that the students are constantly looking to me for advice and a way to find answers to our environmental crisis; and the more I think about it, the fewer answers I seem to have.

At the end of this semester, however, I presented an experiment to the class that seemed to make sense. I had them place a number of trash items on the ground in the hallway and then watch, hidden from view, to see if passersby would pick them up. Keep in mind this is an environmental-based post-secondary institute, so we were betting on good results. Rolls of paper, soda cans, juice boxes and basic garbage were completely ignored by everyone. Money wasn't, though. I placed money in the hallway and it took

The intrinsic value of wilderness has nothing to do with economics, which is why it's the most important value of all.

The Four Senses

Sight is perceived to be the most obvious of the five senses used while in the outdoors. However, studies show that what makes you crave another camping trip is not sight at all; it's the other four senses — smell, taste, touch and sound.

Most memorable (good and bad) camping smells

- wet canvas
- pine needles
- wood smoke
- suntan lotion
- lip balm
- newly constructed outhouse
- overused outhouse
- baked bannock
- camp coffee
- Canadian bacon
- wet dog
- dirty socks
- damp wool sweater
- mayfly exoskeletons rotting below a rapid
- spring flowers
- autumn leaves
- bug spray
- duct tape
- fox pee
- chili, and the resulting silent but deadly toots
- fish fillets frying in oil
- peeled onions
- fresh snow
- morning rain
- the air seconds after a lightening strike
- single malt scotch in an enamel cup
- body odor after wearing a rubber rain jacket during an all-day downpour
- burnt marshmallows

Memorable sounds

- spring peepers at dusk
- call of the whip-o-wills
- laugh of the pileated woodpecker (used to depict Woody Woodpecker's laugh)
- two porcupines mating — seriously, it sounds like a wailing banshee
- crackling of a campfire
- scream of a red-tail hawk, which, by the way, has always been used by Disney to depict the call of an eagle
- echo of a paddle hitting the side of a Grumman canoe
- slap of a beaver's tail
- barred owl calling "Who-cooks-for-you, Who-cooks-for-you-all"
- rain on the tarp
- loons laughing in the morning
- wolves howling in the evening
- children giggling in the tent just before bed time
- leaves rustling in the wind
- leaves rustling beside you on the hiking trail!
- waves lapping against the rockbound shore
- roar of upcoming rapids
- distant thunder
- raven's croak-like call
- mosquitoes buzzing outside the tent
- red squirrel scolding you from above
- silence

Memorable tastes

- melted butter on fresh bannock
- first sip of morning coffee
- first and last sip of brandy
- hot tea
- mini-marshmallows soaked in hot chocolate

- northwest wind
- sand
- seconds of dessert
- a chocolate bar found on day 10 at the bottom of the food pack, one you didn't know you had
- fresh fish

- clean, cold water
- fresh blueberries
- fiddle heads
- bad smoked oyster
- black fly in your chardonnay
- tofu chunks soaked in soy sauce

Memorable touch

- sand on bare feet
- soft moss
- smooth rocks
- slimy fish
- squashed mosquito
- dry kindling
- well-worn paddle shaft
- sunrise on tent wall after a cold night
- perfect snowball
- contents of milkweed pod
- white pine needles

- burrs
- cozy camp chair
- fluffy down sleeping bag
- wet boots on a cold morning
- dry socks
- swamp ooze
- a helping hand
- driftwood
- night air
- warmth of a campfire
- toasted marshmallow stuck on fingers

- snuggle from child
- morning dip in the lake
- surprise flip in the rapids
- sting of a pine beetle
- bad fall on sharp rocks
- brushing up against raspberry bush
- stinging nettle
- sunburn
- cool wet bandana
- can of cold pop (or beer) after the trip

A marshmallow toasted on a stick, burnt or not, is definitely a memorable taste.

Alana settles down to read a good book at one of our "secret spots" we've been going to for years; it's a special place we like to call our own.

no longer than ten seconds for a quarter to be grabbed and a mere three-and-a-half seconds for a two-dollar coin. My conclusion — make garbage worth money and you have your environmental crisis solved.

This, of course, sounds reasonable. But remember, I've been teaching this course for almost twenty years. The garbage into money is not a new idea. The experiment may have made the majority of students happy and had them believe that there was a clear answer to the problem; but it made me more depressed about our outlook than ever before.

The problem, as I see it, is "how" we value wilderness areas. Many textbooks on the subject have a list of taxonomic values we can use. This system is a good clear way to view what we think of as identifiable dimensions we can set forth to protect natural areas. The drawback, however, is that the first value on the list, and what's perceived as the most important by the majority of people, is always market value, followed by life support, recreational, genetic... Sadly, last on the list is always intrinsic value. This is a value that can't be measured in a cost-benefit analysis. What I mean is, it can't be easily explained by placing garbage and money in the hallway to be picked up by passers by. Money has nothing to do with intrinsic values.

Intrinsic values are the least anthropocentric criteria listed, that is, the ones least considering humans the center of the universe, and therefore the most difficult to quantify or define; yet paradoxically, they are among the most important to consider in order to protect areas for us to camp and get away from it all. These are values that become clear the moment a loon wails across a misty lake; when a wolf howls at the moon. Intrinsic value is in the idea that a single pine cone has the capacity to replant an entire forest; or the philosophy that says a grizzly has the right to exist simply because it exists. These values can never have a dollar price set to them, but if they are not respected, we'll become the poorest people imaginable.

THAT SPECIAL PLACE

In nature, one never really sees a thing for the first time until one has seen it for the fiftieth.

— Joseph Wood Krutch

If you are lucky, you have a spot in the woods you like to call your own. A "secret spot" that you return to time and time again, either alone or with best friends and family — all of whom are sworn to confidentiality.

Mine is a small pond not far from where I live. It's nothing special, just a cozy corner in a vast woodland. There's a rustic campsite on the southeast corner of the pond, a perfect spot that gets both sunrise and sunset. It's not the most scenic wonder or known for its natural beauty; it's more of a refuge for me and whoever wants to share it with me.

A Perfect Campsite...

- Faces west-southwest to catch the morning light and the last rays of the evening glow,
- Is exposed enough to allow the wind keep the bugs back but with enough trees to protect you from harsh winds,
- Has a tent site in the shade (but not under an aging tree that could come crashing down during a storm) and not set in a hollow or low area in case of flooding,
- Has a good source of clean water nearby,
- Has a good supply of firewood and the fire ring is set on bedrock so there's no danger of tree roots igniting,
- Has a swimming hole,
- Has no stagnant water around to attract mosquitoes,
- And...is not taken by any other camper.

I've gone there to think about my past, and my future. I go there to release my stress at work and to rethink the present. I went there a couple of days after my father died and a couple of days before my daughter was born. I even spent Christmas Eve there once, after having enough of all the consumer hype, family politics and overindulgence. And I've gone to my special place whenever I feel blessed about the treasures given to me in my life.

What better place to go and reflect on life? I think that's why we truly do love camping in wild areas. Eventually, the more you camp, the more your life spent roaming the woods becomes a comfort. There's nothing better for the soul than an oasis.

This all came clear to me a couple of years ago when my father was in a coma. In between visits to the hospital, regular life, and trying to decide whether to embark on a preplanned one-month canoe trip in familiar Quetico park, I broke out in a nasty rash. My doctor told me the rash was due to stress (big surprise) and that the only way to rid myself of the skin irritation was to relax. Yeah, right, I thought.

As it turned out, my father woke up from the coma the day before my departure date and told me to go on my trip. And three days into the trip my rash miraculously disappeared. But the day the trip was over and I began driving back home, the rash came back. So, you see, I have to conclude that if visiting a familiar place in the wilderness can take a rash away, it's definitely good for the soul.

CAMPFIRES

I like to sing, I love to dance
I'd play the fool if I got the chance,
All around the campfire light
All around the campfire light.

— Ian Tamblyn,
"Campfire Light, Days of Sun and Wind"

It was a sad day when our local Scout leader plugged the "campfire" bulb into the socket of the church basement. He had good intentions; I'll give him that. He was attempting to recreate the atmosphere of a real campfire ring after he had to cancel our annual campout due to a lack of volunteers. But the desperate act of using a red light bulb rather than the real thing was the beginning of the end for me. I dropped out of Scouts and joined the local soccer team.

What is it about campfires? Why are they so vivid in our memories of camping out? The flickering light, sparks spiraling into the night sky, the warmth radiating from the inner circle. To say the appeal of a campfire is that it gives us warmth and light would be correct, but that is certainly not the whole reason. It may be that it connects all of us to our primitive times when our ancestors depended dearly upon the heat it generated for pure survival. But circling a fire ring with green sticks poked through puffy marshmallow can't relate back to our primordial instincts. Again, it has to be much more than that.

Flame Facts

- At its peak a campfire reaches a temperature of approximately 900° F (480° C). That's hot enough to melt down soft metals such as lead or zinc but too cool to bake a clay pot.

- The color of flames is derived from its soot, which when heated becomes incandescent, and in return gives off thermal radiation in the form of light. The coolest portion of the flame is red and the hottest bluish-white.

- Fuel (wood) in the fire also influences the color of a campfire; the more sodium, the more light will be emitted.

- A minute segment of a flame is plasma, which is an odd state of matter that's similar to a gas but doesn't behave like one. That's the part that seems to mesmerize most campers as they watch the flames dancing around as the wood burns down to embers.

Eureka's new collapsible firebox helps you practice no-trace camping but still allows you to enjoy the comforts of an evening fire.

Campfires do give us a great sense of community. Whether there are two or ten people circling it, the ones involved in this simple act are able to connect and discuss issues of the world more easily than at a coffee shop or sitting on a barstool back home.

Sociability isn't the sole reason, though. Solo travelers enjoy a campfire just as much as a group of people, even more so, actually. It gives them a sense of security, nightly entertainment and a feeling of calm.

Actually, I think it's the feeling of calm that's the biggest benefit. Campfires give us a lot of pleasures but the very idea of sitting around a campfire is what signifies that you've finally begun to slow down. Your senses open up. A campfire starts to sound good, look good and smell good. You can distinctively hear the snap of exploding resin, watch as the flames change color as it absorbs oxygen, and smell the woodsmoke rising from logs of maple, birch or pine.

"Chop your own wood and it will warm you twice." The citation, derived from Henry David Thoreau's famous dictum on the subject of pleasures of wood gathering, is inscribed above Camp Kooch-i-ching's mantel. Edward Abbey noted the pleasure as well. He exulted in the act of gathering up desert juniper to kindle the campfire. Since I've never been to the desert, my favorite literary statement about wood gathering is that made by Sigurd Olson. His choice for fueling a fire was the weathered pine knots

"Chop your own wood and it will warm you twice." Henry David Thoreau.

I Hate White Rabbits

Remember, wherever there's smoke, there's fire.

I recall the first time I heard the phrase "I hate white rabbits" being yelled out around the fire ring to chase the smoke away. It seemed more than a little odd. But the moment smoke made a move toward me at my next campfire, I belted out the silly chant almost immediately. And it worked. The smoke drifted over to the next person in our group. It's as if I had some kind of supernatural powers or something. That moment solidified a firm belief since then I've used the phrase on a regular basis. But does it have any merit? Well. . . . It seems the whole thing originated from the idea that white rabbits were considered an omen of death and that in England good luck would come upon you if you called out "white rabbit" three times on the first of every month. The poor white bunnies have been cursed every since.

of Canadian Shield country: "In the fall, I like to gather these blackened old nuggets of energy so that I have a good supply for the long winter evenings ahead. They are far too precious to burn often, and only on special occasions, when a fine bed of coals has formed and friends are sitting around talking and laughing in its glow, do I bring one in, push it carefully into the waiting embers."

It must be noted that the only true way to know what fuel works and where to get it is for you to know your surroundings. I camp a lot near my home in Peterborough, Ontario. It's part of what's called the Great Lakes Forest Region. And my favorite fuel for an evening fire in that area is dead and dried maple, oak or iron wood. It's a piece that's too old to be considered a sapling but too young to be mature. If you're lucky you'll come across ones still standing, the ones that can easily be pushed down, dragged back to camp, and sawed up into arm-size pieces. When cut up and burned, this wood has an extended flame time, great for cooking or just keeping the chill out during a ghost story or two. It also stacks well and is a welcome sight for anyone using the camp after you.

LIVING PRIMITIVELY

The longing to be primitive is a disease of culture.
— George Santayana, *Little Essays*

At times I don't necessarily understand the notion behind trying to survive in the wilds. After all, if it's true what the experts say, that mental fortitude far outweighs physical abilities while battling the elements, then wouldn't the intelligent thing to do be not get yourself in trouble in the first place?

Homemade Fire Starters

- A cotton ball dipped in Vaseline and stored in a waterproof container
- A strip of inner tube
- A ball of steel wool
- Strips of wax paper
- Pieces of wax crayon

- Birthday candles or tealights
- Sawdust or dryer lint dipped in paraffin and stored in an egg carton
- Roll of duct tape coated with a few squirts of bug repellent (this is my favorite)
- Squirt of alcohol-based hand sanitizer

Intellect aside, however, it seems everyone has a strong desire to, at least once, try testing their survival skills. It may be that we're all just bored of our modern lifestyle. Or it might be that we have a hidden urge to feel what it would be like to live like our ancestors. It could also be that we are so far removed from wilderness at this point in our development that it's necessary to somehow feel the connection with nature that we once had — and living primitively definitely does the trick.

Whatever the reason, I recently decided to give it a go. It was planned, of course. I created a fake scenario by simply driving to a wooded area not far from my home and walked half-an-hour into the bush. Time spent would be four nights and I was armed with only a small survival kit consisting of simple things like a pocket knife and fishing line. My wife also insisted that I take a water filter to treat my water, a butane lighter in case the stick rubbing didn't go as planned and a couple of chocolate bars in case the hunger thing got out of control.

The spot where I chose to camp out was a small pond located just far enough from the road that traffic couldn't be heard. It wasn't ideal, I guess. But the important point is that no one knew I was there (except for my wife).

Following a pocket-size survival manual I packed along, I did the first thing the book suggested. Build a shelter. And upon completion it resembled a pile of forest debris more than an actual shelter. But the heap of sticks interlaced with conifer boughs became crucial very quickly. A cold drizzle started shortly after I had completed the lean-to type structure and it didn't stop raining until the second-last day of the trip.

Fire was next on the manual's list and I spent a good couple of hours attempting to ignite my pile of wood just outside the shelter with a makeshift bow-drill. The work it required kept me warm at first. But with the rain continuing to pour down, and me having no natural skill whatsoever, it soon became apparent how ludicrous it was to start a fire this way. So I pulled out the butane lighter my wife had forced me to pack along and ignited a very welcomed campfire.

At this point, the only true element of survival that I had felt was the constant feeling of being cold and hungry. It was only a few hours into it and already I wanted desperately to be rescued. How embarrassing it would be to be found dead while faking a survival exercise a half-hour away from my vehicle. A smidgen of pride and the prospect of my wife tell me "I told you so" when I got home were the only things that kept me from packing it in and walking back the highway

Shamefully I ate the first of the two chocolate bars and curled up in the fetal position under my crude shelter for the night, declaring to start off fresh in the morning.

Waking up in the morning without the scent of brewed coffee to entice me was a real test. How primal tribes ever survived without morning coffee is beyond me. I did make use of the water filter, however — the pond was

How embarrassing it would be to need rescuing while faking a survival exercise at a semi-wilderness spot just a half hour away from my vehicle.

How to Light a One-Match Fire

Starting the evening fire with just one match is the most critical challenge given to a group of campers. It beats catching the biggest fish or carrying the heaviest load. On my annual spring fishing trips with friends the bets are on for getting the fire going and the stakes get higher the fouler the weather. It's a gamble but the rules are that if you are able to get a fire going with just one match, during a persistent all-day rain, then you win another group member's full flask of rum. Here's how I manage to win most of the wagers.

- Go far back behind camp to collect a handful of dead and dry pencil-sized twigs under the canopy of evergreen trees.

- Locate a downed tree and saw off the end not touching the ground (wood touching the ground will quickly rot) with one of those collapsible camp-saws into pieces no greater than the length and thickness of my arm.

- Use thin strips of birch bark, dry pine needles, a glob of pitch squeezed from balsam blisters or a piece of dried lichen as a fire starter; or use a homemade fire starter (see page 230) and place it at base of the fire ring.

- Place the pencil-size twigs in a criss-cross pattern over the fire-starter material.

- Place the larger pieces on top but make sure there's plenty of space for the fire to breathe (too much smoke means you're smothering the flames).

- Place a few more pencil-sized twigs on top to lock everything in place.

- Ignite the fire-starter material with a match stored in a waterproof container (to make sure the match is dry, place a cotton ball on top of the matches in the container and briskly run the match through your hair before igniting it to draw out any moisture).

- Construct a second pile of wood around and even on top of the fire to constantly dry out your fuel source.

A one-match fire.

somewhat murky, almost stagnant — and then spent a good part of the morning fixing my leaky shelter and gathering more wood for the fire. I even made a serious attempt at catching a fish with the line, hook and sinker from the survival kit — with no luck, of course.

How frustrating that was. I had caught plenty of bass and pike in the same pond on previously outings. Mind you, that was with a graphite rod, open-face reel and a huge selection of tackle. Throwing out a piece of line baited with a squashed deerfly just didn't cut it. Midafternoon I gave in to my hunger and ate my second chocolate bar.

The second night's sleep was next to impossible, although not necessarily due to the confined space of the shelter or my hunger pains. I had weird dreams, storylines that dealt with past girlfriends, high school bullies and the death of my father.

In a foggy state I crawled out of the shelter in the early morning light and gave fishing another try, this time using a frog as bait. On my third toss I caught a bass around the same size as the frog, and for breakfast I ate both the fish and the frog.

Pieces of my morning catch caught me another bass for lunch, but dinner was cattail shoots and a handful of late-season blueberries that resembled miniature raisins more than plump berries. I could have made an attempt at snaring a squirrel or tossing a rock at a ruffed grouse. The decision was made before my trip, however, that it wouldn't be ethical (or legal, for that matter) to kill a more protein-enriched species other than a fish (the frog was consumed in desperation). Not that I wouldn't if this survival epic was real. I'd probably eat what ever moved out there.

Before nightfall I attempted to fish once again and caught nothing. My bad luck had much to do with the fact that my decreased energy made me throw the line out like a sissy. At this point I felt dizzy and lethargic. But I also felt somewhat triumphant, even survivalistic, if there is such a thing. I was upbeat, which according to my manual was the most important element to have at this point in the game. I knew, of course, that come morning I was free to walk back to my vehicle and speed toward the nearest fast-food joint. That said, however, my body and mind had still managed to get a taste of what it would be like to survive in the wilderness. My inner perspective was certainly heightened and my awareness of the natural surroundings was surreal. I may have questioned putting myself in such a predicament but at least I felt my animal instincts finally kick in.

I was able to pick up on the slightest movement in the woods — the sound of a chattering squirrel, a songbird fluttering through camp, a fish slurping a bug off the surface of the pond. Mind you, my senses likely peaked because I wanted to eat all the critters moving around out there. But I did feel totally primitive and very much connected to nature — connected rather than conquering — and I liked that. I liked it a lot.

WILDERNESS AND THE ART OF DECEPTION

I've dabbled in the art of canoe cinematography for a few years now, and let me tell you, it is tough work. Last year, while filming in Quetico, I got to know the pain all too well. Capturing scene after scene is a daunting task all on its own, but add on all the discomforts of canoe travel on top of that and the process can be mind-numbing. On day seven of our eight-day trip I crashed. I was paddling solo while the filmmaker (Kip) and assistant (Andy) paddled in a tandem boat. It had already been a long day of paddling big windy lakes and humping over a few grueling portages, so when Kip asked to capture one last scene of me paddling across a full moon shining across the expanse of Quetico's Pickerel Lake, I rebelled and said no!

Kip is a professional, however. He's been in the filming business a long time and has seen a lot of mutinous behavior. I don't even recall him trying to talk me out of it. He placed my hat and PFD on Andy, mandating him to paddle out and complete the scene, and when the film aired you couldn't tell the difference. The audio was later muted (Kip dubbed in a few loon calls), so you couldn't even hear me yelling at him.

So you see, filming wilderness can be slightly dishonest at times, especially with the high-tech gear used nowadays. That last evening in Quetico, we poured a double shot of rum into our camp mugs, and then used up the remainder of the camera battery to view all the footage Kip had got throughout the trip. It was odd. Here we were watching our work on site, on the screen of a high-definition digital camera complete with computerized editing suite. We couldn't image what poor Ken Buck, Bill Mason's camera-man, had to go through during their filming excursions back in the 1970s and 80s when they produced *Path of the Paddle, Song of the Paddle* and *Waterwalker* using only a 16 mm camera. The technology of the time meant that the footage couldn't be viewed until weeks after the trip.

During our screening session, however, it also became obvious to us that the wilderness part of what we caught on camera during our trip hadn't altered one little bit from when Ken and Bill roamed around doing the same thing. We felt as if we had been true to the wild; as Bill Mason himself said after filming *Waterwalker:* "Film can be deceiving… But when it comes to the beauty of the world out here, the camera has not lied."

Camping life is full of the simplest pleasures. Madawaska River, Ontario.

Alana and I are truly blessed to have a daughter like Kyla who loves to camp.

BIBLIOGRAPHY

Arnold, Kevin. "The Light Stuff." *Explore* magazine, March 2005.

Bell, Patricia J. *Roughing it Elegantly.* Eden Prairie, Minnesota: Cat's-paw Press, 1994.

Bennet, Doug and Tim Tiner. *Up North.* Markham, Ontario: Reed Books Canada, 1993.

Cruchet, Matt. "Finding Your Waypoint." *CanoeRoots,* Spring 2007.

Dennis, Jerry. *From a Wooden Canoe.* New York: St. Martin's Press, 1999.

Dillman, Erika. *Outdoors Online.* Seattle, WA: The Mountaineers Books, 2007.

Dorn, Jonathan. "Ultralight Made Easy." *Backpacker,* December 2002.

Grady, Wayne. "Walking Like a Human." *Explore* magazine, October 2002.

Greenspan, Rick and Hal Kahn. *The Camper's Companion.* San Francisco: Foghorn Press, 1991.

Jacobson, Cliff. *Camping Secrets.* Merrillville, Indiana: ICS Books Inc., 1987.

Jacobson, Cliff. *Canoeing and Camping Beyond the Basics.* Merrillville, Indiana: ICS Books Inc., 1992.

Jacobson, Cliff. *Canoeing Wild Rivers.* Merrillville, Indiana: ICS Books Inc., 1992.

Jacobson, Cliff. "Then and Now." *Kanawa* magazine, Summer 2007.

Jenkins, Mary. "The Warm Side of the Coldest Season." *Backpacker,* October 1993.

Kimber, Robert. *A Canoeist's Sketchbook.* Post Mills, Vermont: Chelsea Green Publishing Company, 1991.

Kraiker, Rolf and Debra. *Cradle to Canoe.* Erin: Boston Mills Press, 1999.

Little, James. "125 Things We Love Out There." *Explore* magazine, June 2006.

Little, James. "100 Years of Outdoor Recreation in Canada." *Explore* magazine, November 1999.

Macfarlane, David. "Honour the Fire." *Cottage Life,* August 2007.

Mahaffey, Dexter. "Green Gear." *Paddler* magazine, November 2006.

Mason, Bill. *Song of the Paddle.* Toronto: Key Porter Books, 1988.

Matthews, Rick. "Shooting the Setting Sun." *CanoeRoots,* Summer 2005.

Mears, Ray. *Bushcraft.* London: Hodder & Stoughton, 2002.

Miller, Nancy Baren. "The joys of RVing: recreation vehicles open up new horizon." *Travel America,* June 2005.

Noah, Timothy. "You Are How You Camped." *State* magazine, July 2006.

Scriver, Mark. "Come on Baby." *CanoeRoots,* Summer 2007.

Stuhaug, Dennis. "Explore the Classic Gear of Canoe Camping." *Canoe Journal,* 2001.

Townsend, Chris and Annie Aggens. *Encyclopedia of Outdoor and Wilderness Skills.* Camden, ME: Ragged Mountain Press, 2003.

Websites

www.backpacking.net, "Lightening the Load," Greg Cope

www.backpacking.net, "The Philosophy and Practice of Traveling Light in the Backcountry," Charles Lindsay

www.CNN.com, "Luxury Camping; roughing it the easy way"

www.cocktails.about.com/od/cocktailrecipes/r/algnqn_ckctl.htm

www.extreme-planet.com/news.asp

www.forbestraveler.com, "21st-Century Camping," Stephen Regenold

www.geocities.com/suarezgfam/SmoresHistory.html

www.gorp.away.com/gorp/interact/topten/cds.htm, "Top Ten CDs to take RVing"

www.paddling.net, "It's Only Natural," Tamia Nelson

www.pcthiker.com, "How to Make a Pepsi Stove"

www.myccr.com, "Best Whiskey for Tripping"

www.nationalgeographic.com/pathtoadventure/handbook/survival/survival5.html

www.nessmuking.com/ado.htm

www.solarnavigator.net/history/great_explorers.htm

www.solotripping.com/

www.treehugger.com/files/2007/06/how-to-green-your-outdoor-sports.php

INDEX